Nikolai Maksimenko

Fundamentals of anti-corruption culture. Course of lectures

Nikolai Maksimenko

Fundamentals of anti-corruption culture. Course of lectures

For students of higher educational institutions

ScienciaScripts

Imprint
Any brand names and product names mentioned in this book are subject to trademark, brand or patent protection and are trademarks or registered trademarks of their respective holders. The use of brand names, product names, common names, trade names, product descriptions etc. even without a particular marking in this work is in no way to be construed to mean that such names may be regarded as unrestricted in respect of trademark and brand protection legislation and could thus be used by anyone.

Cover image: www.ingimage.com

This book is a translation from the original published under ISBN 978-613-4-91711-7.

Publisher:
Sciencia Scripts
is a trademark of
Dodo Books Indian Ocean Ltd. and OmniScriptum S.R.L publishing group

120 High Road, East Finchley, London, N2 9ED, United Kingdom
Str. Armeneasca 28/1, office 1, Chisinau MD-2012, Republic of Moldova, Europe
Printed at: see last page
ISBN: 978-620-8-09901-5

CONTENTS

INTRODUCTION

Nowadays, corruption is one of the most important problems of the world community. Its destructive impact on society is universal. According to various estimates only direct economic losses from corruption, for example, in Russia are from 20 to 40 billion dollars a year, which is comparable to the income of the state budget of the country, and the volume of bribes to Russian officials, according to the National Anti-Corruption Committee of the Russian Federation, is from 240 to 300 billion dollars and this figure is growing.

Corruption hinders business development, exacerbates social inequality, and makes formally free public services (education, medicine, etc.) difficult to access for the least well-off segments of the population. It decomposes the political system, distorting the goals of social development, and contributes to political instability. As a consequence of ineffective governance, corruption makes it even more ineffective.

The topic of corruption is also relevant for modern Kazakhstan. Our country is one of the most corrupt countries in the world. According to the International non-governmental organization Transparency International[1] the corruption perception index of Kazakhstan in 2016 was 29 points out of 100, ranking 131st out of 176 countries, behind such countries of the former Soviet Union as Moldova and Azerbaijan (both with 30 points), Armenia (33), Belarus (40), Georgia and Latvia (both 57), Lithuania (59), Estonia (70). The amounts of individual bribes in our country in 2015 reached $500,000; only in seven months of this year the number of corruption offenses reached 1,728 cases[2] . O. Abdykarimov, Chairman of the Republican Public Council on Combating Corruption under the People's Democratic Party "Nur Otan", deputy of the Senate of the Parliament of the Republic of Kazakhstan, noted: "Corruption hinders healthy competition. It leads to the adoption of unjustified decisions that do not contribute to the optimal use of resources. It reduces the competitiveness of Kazakhstan's economy compared to the economic systems of countries where the level of corruption is lower and the level of transparency is higher. Corruption contributes to an increase in crime rates, especially an increase in the level of organized crime and the shadow economy. Opacity and corruption of the economic system create an environment that destroys public morality and contributes to the loss of confidence of citizens in the rule of law. And such confidence is one of the most important bases for creating conditions for economic growth"[3] .

Corruption is described in the media as a serious barrier to the healthy development of society, a social evil that requires intervention and elimination. Among the most corrupt institutions are[4] state authorities, local authorities, law enforcement agencies, courts, traffic police, public utilities, political parties, and the media. In the social sphere, health care, education, conscription into the army, bribes have become commonplace to resolve an issue.

---

1 http://www.forbes.ru/news/248161-rossiya-sokhranila-pozitsii-v-reitinge-vospriyatiya-korruptsii
2 https://news.mail.ru/inworld/kazakhstan/incident/22999704/?frommail= 1
3 The art of demanding sacrifices. Express-K" newspaper. No. 48 (17406) of 16.03.2012
4 See www.transparency.org.ru.

But the effective fight against this negative phenomenon is impossible without a sufficiently complete and accurate knowledge of its essence, specific conditions of occurrence and consequences.

Therefore, it is not by chance that two years ago a course "Fundamentals of anti-corruption culture" was introduced in all higher educational institutions of Kazakhstan. And today we proceed to the systematic study of this course and the topic of today's class: "Social and legal essence and main causes of corruption. Types of corruption".

TOPIC 1. SOCIAL AND LEGAL ESSENCE AND MAIN CAUSES OF CORRUPTION. TYPES OF CORRUPTION

Plan

1. The concept of corruption as a social phenomenon.
2. Content and types of corrupt relations.
3. Causes of corruption and its social consequences.
4. Corruption in Kazakhstan.

1. Concept of corruption as a social phenomenon

Corruption is a complex, ambiguous concept perceived by different people, which is historical in nature and largely depends on the social conditions and traditions of a particular country. The most adequate understanding of corruption is possible only by taking into account social attitudes, perceptions and stereotypes of consciousness of the population of a given country or region, as well as its emotional perception.

In Soviet times, bribery was synonymous with corruption, which is quite understandable, since for most citizens in those conditions bribery was the only form of corruption in which they or their relatives, acquaintances or colleagues were involved.

However, with the transition of the former Soviet republics to market relations, with the provision of citizens with the opportunity to own any property, with the development of monetary circulation and securities market, the greatest losses for society and the state began to be caused by corrupt transactions related to the misuse of budget funds and their redistribution, underpayment of taxes, etc., which pushed bribery into the background. Here bribes remained in relations between citizens and businessmen and officials; as for high-ranking government officials, they have more opportunities to receive multimillion-dollar illegal incomes without resorting to bribes and without violating the law. For example, on formally legal grounds, to grant a tender for a favorable supply of equipment to a firm owned by the official's spouse.

As already mentioned, the understanding of corruption is largely determined by national, ethnic, religious and legal traditions, which allow for attributing or not attributing certain actions to corruption. For example, in some countries, giving a gift to a superior on the occasion of his or her birthday is considered normal, while in other countries it is perceived as a gross violation of ethical norms.

Thus, on the one hand, corruption manifests itself in violation of social norms, ethical deviations in behavior, and, on the other hand, it manifests itself in the use by officials of their status to obtain illegal benefits, or in providing such benefits to other officials or citizens who do not hold positions. It can manifest itself in direct theft of state or public values (money, material resources, etc.).

Many corrupt actions are carried out within the framework of the powers granted to officials, and it is not always possible to legally prove their personal benefit related to these actions, i.e. formally carried out without violating the law. This has led many researchers to the conclusion that "countering corruption solely through criminal prosecution of officials is ineffective for the purpose of reducing the overall level of corruption"[5] . In other words, modern definitions of corruption do not directly link it only to criminal offenses, but do not exclude such possibilities.

Until recently, corruption as a social phenomenon was the subject of close attention only to legal scholars and was reduced, as already mentioned, mainly to bribery. However, the widespread spread of corruption today and its penetration into all spheres of public life have led researchers to realize its multifaceted and multidimensional nature. As modern society and the state develop, corruption is becoming more and more diverse, so it can be described and studied from different perspectives. There are four main approaches to understanding corruption in modern literature[6] .

1. **Legal interpretation of corruption.** Lawyers understand corruption as a crime related to the use of official position or social status of a public official for personal or corporate purposes. Most often such interest is reduced to obtaining illegal income in the form of receiving or giving bribes. In this case, bribes, along with money, securities and other property, may be services of a non-property nature, rendered free of charge, but subject to payment (travel vouchers, repair of apartments, construction of houses or summer residences, etc.). Understatement of the value of privatized objects, reduction of rent, interest rates for the use of bank loans, etc. are considered bribes.

2. **Economic understanding of corruption.** Corruption here means the activities of business, state or municipal officials that cause financial and resource losses for business, the state, individual communities, and the development of the country as a whole. In this approach, the danger of corruption is assessed by the level of financial losses resulting from corrupt practices.

3. **Understanding corruption from the perspective of governance.** In this approach, corruption is understood as an action that disrupts or destroys normal state or municipal governance enshrined in regulations and laws, leading to its systemic inefficiency due to the fact that personal or corporate interests begin to prevail over state and public interests.

4. **Sociological understanding of corruption.** From the sociological point of view, corruption is the use of informal ties and relations in solving political, state and municipal problems for personal or corporate interests. Procedures for solving such problems are associated with **favoritism** and **clientelism,** especially in the area of personnel decisions and subsequent assistance to the officials who thus received their appointments.

Each of the four approaches reveals a separate aspect of corruption, but together they provide a fairly complete characterization of the essence of this phenomenon.

The term corruption itself comes from the combination of the Latin words "correi"

---

5 State policy of counteraction to corruption and shadow economy in Russia. Materials of the All-Russian Scientific Conference (Moscow, June 6, 2007). - M., 2007. C.179.

6 See: State policy of countering corruption and shadow economy in Russia. Materials of the All-Russian Scientific Conference (Moscow, June 6, 2007). - M., 2007. C. 179-180.

(several persons bound by an obligation regarding one object) and "rumpere" (to break, damage, undo). As a result, an independent term was formed, which implies the involvement of several (at least two) persons whose purpose was to break (spoil) or damage the normal course of the judicial process or the process of managing certain affairs of society.

As for the definition of this phenomenon, there are many definitions of it in scientific, educational and public-public literature. The explanatory dictionary of the Russian language characterizes corruption as bribery, venality of officials and political figures.

The UN reference document on the international fight against corruption defines the latter as "the abuse of public power for private gain".

It includes bribery (giving a reward to corrupt a person out of a position of duty), nepotism (replacing lucrative or lucrative positions with relatives or "one's own people" through patronage) and misappropriation of public funds for private use.

The Law of the Russian Federation "On Combating Corruption" defines corruption as "abuse of official position, bribery, bribe-giving, bribe-taking, abuse of authority, commercial bribery or other unlawful use by an individual of his or her official position contrary to the legitimate interests of society and the state in order to obtain a benefit in the form of money, valuables, other property or services of a property nature, other property rights for himself or herself or for third parties, or the unlawful provision of such a benefit to the said person.

The Law of the Republic of Kazakhstan "On Combating Corruption" defines it as follows: "Corruption in this Law shall mean the acceptance of property benefits and advantages personally or through intermediaries by persons performing public functions, as well as persons equal to them, not provided for by law, with the use of their official powers and related opportunities, or other use of their powers to obtain a property benefit, as well as bribery of such persons by unlawfully providing them with physical and psychological support, and the use of their powers to obtain a property benefit.

As can be seen from this definition, corruption here refers only to unlawful acts of persons performing public functions or persons equivalent to them, as well as those who attempt to induce them to engage in unlawful acts through bribery.

The Council of Europe experts have developed the following general definition of corruption: "Corruption is bribery, graft and any other conduct by a person vested with responsibilities in the public or private sector which violates his duties arising from his public status as a public person, private employee, independent agent or other status of a similar nature and is aimed at obtaining an undue advantage of any kind for himself or another person"[7] .

A report prepared by the Russian Council on Foreign and Defense Policy and the Indem Regional Public Foundation states that "corruption (in the narrow sense of the word) is

---

7 Some aspects of international legal cooperation of the Council of Europe member states in the field of combating corruption// Journal of Russian Law. 2000, № 7.

understood as a situation when an official makes an illegal decision (sometimes a decision that is morally unacceptable to public opinion) from which some other party benefits (for example, a firm that secures a government order against the established procedure thanks to this decision), while the official himself receives illegal remuneration from the ethical authority of the state Characteristics of this situation: a decision is made that violates the law or unwritten social norms, both parties act with mutual consent, both parties receive illegal benefits and advantages, both parties try to conceal their actions"[8] .

In these two definitions, corruption is defined as a situation in which a public official makes an illegal decision (often morally unacceptable to public opinion) from which some other party benefits, and the official himself receives an illegal reward from this party. In the case of corruption, a decision is made that violates the law or unwritten social norms, both parties act by mutual consent; both parties receive illegal benefits and advantages, both parties try to conceal their actions. These are the definitions we will rely on in the further presentation of the course.

Here is another definition of corruption: corruption is "a social phenomenon characterized by bribery - venality of public or other officials and, on this basis, their selfish use of official official official powers, authority and opportunities associated with them for personal or narrow group or corporate interests"[9] .

2. Content and types of corrupt relations

The content of any phenomenon is characterized by the forms of its existence, which, as it follows from the course of philosophy, determine, first of all, its mode of existence. Everything has a form, and corruption also has a form.

Corruption is possible where there is a person who has the ability to dispose of resources that do not belong to him or her by making or not making certain decisions. When this person is a civil servant, we are dealing with public corruption, which causes the greatest harm to society and the state, as it is related to budget funds, state or municipal property, state orders or benefits, etc.

Since corruption is a two-way relationship, the subjects of corruption relations are, on the one hand, officials and, on the other hand, representatives of the legal and illegal private sector, or individuals.

The object of corruption may be practically all social and economic relations established and protected by law.

Modern literature considers corruption to be a complex criminological, socio-economic phenomenon with a multistructured and multilevel content and associated with a complex of heterogeneous types of socially dangerous acts. It manifests itself in all spheres of public life.

8 Satarov G.A., Levin M.I. Russia and corruption: who is who? // Rossiyskaya Gazeta. 1998. February 19. P.4.
9 A. Yu. Epikhin O. B. Mozokhin. VChK-OGPU in the fight against corruption in the years of new economic policy (1921-1928). - M., 2007. C. 171.

There are many classifications of types of corruption according to various criteria. The most widespread of them is the division into two main forms: grassroots, lower (petty, everyday, everyday) and apex, higher (elite, large-scale). The most dangerous and the most widespread is corruption in power structures associated with the use of administrative resources.

The appeal of grassroots corruption is that it has value not only for the recipient (or extortionist) of the bribe, but also for the bribe-giver. The bribe helps to solve everyday problems that arise constantly, and it also serves as a small payment for the constant possibility of committing minor violations of laws and regulations (e.g. traffic rules). Low-level corruption creates favorable conditions for the existence of apex corruption, accustoming the population to the view of corruption as a commonplace phenomenon accepted "by default" by a significant part of society.

Here is another classification of types of corruption[10] .

1. Depending on the subject of corruption abusing the position of authority:
- state corruption (corruption of state officials);
- commercial corruption (corruption of firm managers);
- political corruption (corruption of politicians).
2. Depending on the subject of corruption who initiates corrupt relations:
- requesting (extorting) bribes at the initiative of an official;
- bribery at the initiative of the petitioner.
3. Depending on the subject of corruption who is the bribe-giver:
- Individual bribe (on the part of the citizen);
- entrepreneurial bribery (by a legitimate firm);
- Criminal bribery (by criminal entrepreneurs - e.g. drug mafia).
4. Depending on the form of benefit received by the bribe taker from corruption:
- cash bribes;
- exchange of services (patronage, nepotism).
5. Depending on the degree of centralization of corrupt relations:
- decentralized corruption (each bribe-giver acts on his own initiative);
- Bottom-up centralized corruption (bribes regularly collected by lower-level officials are shared between them and more senior officials);
- Top-down centralized corruption (bribes regularly collected by top officials are partially passed on to their subordinates).
6. Depending on the level of prevalence of corrupt relations:

10 See: http://www.webkursovik.ru/kartgotrab.asp?id=-96585

- grassroots corruption (in the lower and middle echelons of power);
- Top-level corruption (of top officials and politicians);
- international corruption (in the sphere of global economic relations).

7. Depending on the degree of regularity of corrupt links:

- occasional corruption;
- systematic (institutional) corruption;
- kleptocracy (corruption as an integral component of power relations).

When analyzing corrupt ties, the correct definition of their subjects is very important. And here it is important to pay attention to the fact that in modern conditions private entrepreneurship, own enterprises, joint-stock companies, etc. are widespread, headed by persons who are not employees of the state administration apparatus, but whose actions may well qualify as corruption.

It is clear that most corruption offences are committed by officials, i.e. those who permanently, temporarily or by special authority exercise the functions of a representative of authority or perform organizational, administrative or economic functions in the relevant state and local authorities and institutions.

At the same time, some categories of employees (e.g. teachers and medical workers), not being representatives of state and local authorities, in the exercise of their professional duties (treatment, taking examinations, etc.) perform actions that give rise to rights and obligations for other persons (e.g. assigning a disability group, giving undeservedly high marks in examinations). In these cases, they are also categorized as officials and act as subjects of corruption.

When characterizing corrupt relations in modern literature, the following concepts are often used[11] :

- **State capture** - attempts by entrepreneurs to influence the decisions of different levels and branches of government (business bribes and buys officials and deputies);

- **seizure of business** - establishment of illegal control over business by officials in order to extract administrative rent (officials use administrative resources to put pressure on campaigns), the rent is provided here not by bribes, but by business and income from it;

- **administrative resource**. Administrative resource (AR) - the ability of an official to influence the management of material resources in the vested interests (his own or someone else's). AR usually appears in the form of telephone right, instructions to subordinates, pressure on subordinate structures, formally independent (police, tax inspection, etc.);

- **conflict of interest** (COI) is a situation of contradiction between personal, private, group (departmental, corporate) interests and the interests of the community, the whole society, the state (organization, party). Everyone can get into a conflict of interest

11 See: Mikhail Gorny. Countering Corruption. http://sudanet.ru/node/12110

situation: a doctor, an engineer, a worker, an official, a politician;

- **Corruption Perception Index** (CPI). The index ranks countries and territories on a scale from 0 (highest level of corruption) to 100 (lowest level of corruption).

The most common type of corruption is a **bribe**, which is understood as "material values (objects, money, services, other property benefits) accepted by an official for an action or inaction in the interests of the bribe-giver, which this person could or should have done by virtue of his or her official position"[12] .

There are the following types of bribes:

- **business bribes** - given to an official to accelerate the performance of his/her official duties (e.g., concluding a contract for a favorable supply of goods to the detriment of other competitors offering more favorable terms);

- **inhibitory bribes** - payment for a hidden suspension of action (e.g., suspending a demand for payment of a fine until the statute of limitations expires, which relieves the bribe-giver from liability for supplying substandard goods);

- **direct bribery** - payment for performing an unlawful act (e.g., for information constituting a trade secret) or inaction (e.g., delaying a competing firm's paperwork for the delivery of goods);

- **corrupt intermediary contracts**. "A characteristic (although far from always distinguishable) feature of these transactions, which are often clothed in the form of ordinary civil law contracts - assignments, commissions, consulting, assistance, is the payment by the intermediary of "secret remuneration", or, simply put, bribery of persons who, due to their official position, connections, etc., can influence the adoption of a decision desirable for the principal, for example, on granting him a favorable order, awarding in his favor a public contract sold through a tender, etc.". The principal is understood to be the person on whose behalf the representative acts"[13] .

In the post-Soviet space, direct or veiled combination of positions in the civil service and in non-state commercial structures, provision of direct or indirect services by civil servants to non-state commercial structures for direct or veiled remuneration, provision of certain benefits and advantages to commercial structures are widespread.

While grassroots corruption is widespread and dangerous, the greatest danger to society and the state is the highest corruption related to public expenditures.

In this area, the main types of sources of corrupt enrichment are[14] :

- **investment projects** are largely determined by decisions that top officials make at their discretion. Large investment projects (especially those involving foreign corporations) often involve the transfer of monopoly rights to the winner of the tender, which promises officials particularly large bribes.

- **Public procurement** usually involves selecting the objectively best offer from

12 https://ru.wikipedia.org/wiki/Взятка

13 Cited in: Zotov V. Will the hand of the taker dry up? // Shield and Sword. 1992. C. 14.

14 See: https://ru.wikipedia.org/wiki/Коррупция

several on the basis of a tender, but sometimes an official can ensure that the seller who has promised the highest "commission" ("kickback") from the transaction wins. This is done by limiting participation in the tender, not announcing its rules in full, etc.

- **extra-budgetary accounts** are often created for a legitimate purpose (pension, road funds, etc.) However, in some funds, for example, to help the disabled, revenues may significantly exceed actual expenditures, which stimulates the desire of some officials to embezzle the "surplus". On the contrary, in case of a deficit, officials often decide at their discretion who gets the money in the end, often not without benefit to themselves.

In the judicial system, as well as for officials authorized to consider administrative cases involving the imposition of sanctions (internal affairs bodies, fire supervision bodies, etc.), the sources of corruption are[15] :

- **"forks" in the legislation**. Many norms have soft and hard penalties, allowing the judge to choose between them, which gives the judge an influence on the offender. At the same time, the greater the difference between the upper and lower limits of punishment, the greater the bribe a citizen will be willing to pay;
- **alternative administrative penalty**. There are alternative norms of punishment, for example, a fine or arrest. What distinguishes them from most "forked" norms is not only a wider range of punishments (and, consequently, a stronger motivation for the offender to bribe), but also the fact that justice is carried out by representatives of the executive, not judicial, power;
- **recharacterization of the offence**. Another type of "forks" is the duplication of the composition of the offense in different codes. This opens up opportunities for reclassification of the committed offense in a milder category (for example, from criminal to administrative or civil), or, conversely, in a more serious category. It is often difficult to distinguish between crimes and other offenses due to the vague wording of the legislation, and in such situations judges (or officials) make a decision at their discretion, which opens up opportunities for bribery and extortion;
- **non-monetary losses of citizens**. Some legal norms may cause corruption by imposing non-monetary losses associated with the violation of the law on the individual. Even if the amount of a fine and a bribe for a crime are nominally equal, it may be more profitable for an offender to pay a bribe than to spend time paying the fine or challenging the punishment in court, as mentioned above.

3. Causes of corruption and its social consequences

Corruption as a social phenomenon is extremely diverse and may have different causes in different countries and regions. At the same time, researchers note that these causes are common in states with similar problems and tasks of economic, political and social order. Thus, the following common causes of corruption are named for countries with economies in transition, which is the type of countries that modern Kazakhstan belongs

15 See: https://ru.wikipedia.org/wiki/Коррупция

to[16] : "economic decline, political instability, underdeveloped and imperfect legislation, inefficiency of government institutions, weakness of civil society institutions, lack of strong democratic traditions of corruption".

These reasons also include "the subject type of political culture of the overwhelming majority of the population..., weakness of the judicial system, underdeveloped legal consciousness of the population, disregard for the law in favor of profit, subordination of officials not to the law, but to their superiors and instructions, impunity for violation of the law".

Important reasons for the spread of corruption in the broadest masses in our country are poverty and low level of social security, difficult access to free medical care, lack of real social elevators.

Among the specific reasons contributing to the growth of corruption offenses are: "imperfect market relations in the economy, gaps in legislation, problems in forming the moral position of citizens, bribery in the state apparatus, inefficiency of law enforcement agencies, delaying the consideration of cases by the courts, etc."[17] .

The reasons causing the spread of corruption are both objective and subjective.

The existence of **objective causes of** corruption is related to the complexity and multifaceted nature of the management process of modern society, which is carried out by a network of administrators at various levels, who are endowed with certain powers and necessary resources and act on the basis of special laws and rules. And here the following problems arise.

1. The real life of modern society is diverse, multifaceted and complex to such an extent that it is practically impossible to envisage in laws and regulations all cases and conflicts encountered in practice, and this gives officials the opportunity to make alternative decisions, including those that are favorable to themselves.

2. In practice, laws and regulations lag behind real life - they change much slower than external conditions, which gives officials the opportunity to act at their discretion, deviating from the instructions. Otherwise, the inconsistency of outdated norms and rules with the real situation can slow down or completely stop work. But it also means that an administrator in such a situation can make decisions favorable to himself to the detriment of the business being managed.

3. The complexity and multifaceted nature of modern society makes it impossible to exercise all-encompassing control over the activities of managers at all levels, which often gives them the opportunity to make decisions, including corrupt decisions, independently and uncontrollably.

Thus, the principles of governance in modern society objectively contain a potential opportunity for corruption.

The level of corruption development is also influenced by the quality of laws adopted:

---

16 Mikhail Gorny. Countering Corruption. http://sudanet.ru/node/12110

17 Malikova A. Sh. Causes and conditions contributing to the emergence of corruption. sapanet.ru/Kafedra/Podrazd/malikov.doc

their ambiguity and contradictions create a wide field for officials to make decisions favorable to them.

A number of researchers refer to "low wages in the public sector compared to the private sector" as objective causes of corruption[18] .

In general, if we summarize numerous works devoted to this problem, the main reasons for the spread of corruption in countries in transition, and Kazakhstan, we repeat, belongs to this type of countries, are:

- economic decline;
- political instability;
- imperfect legislation;
- underdevelopment of power institutions and civil society institutions;
- the weakness of democratic traditions;
- the opacity of the government;
- Ineffective public participation in anti-corruption processes.

At the same time, the lack of transparency of the authorities and ineffective public participation in anti-corruption processes are named as the main reasons for this list.

Non-transparency of power is understood as its closedness, absence or restriction of access of the general public to information about the activities of the authorities, about the procedures of making power decisions. Opacity of the authorities is also associated with the difficulty, and, in extreme cases, with the impossibility for the population to influence the authorities.

Corruption is more difficult where the government is transparent. "**Transparency of power** ***is its openness,*** comprehensibility ***and possibility to influence it*** (hereinafter - emphasized by the compiler - N.M.). **Openness** means access (first of all, to information about the activities of the authorities, about the procedures for making and executing power decisions, to the decisions themselves; access to the premises where the authorities are located, etc.). **Understandability** - what is accessible (procedures, decisions) can be understood. **Possibility of influence** - the possibility of using and changing what is accessible and what has become clear (power procedures, information, decisions)"[19] .

Public participation is the participation of the population, various structures of civil society in the preparation, adoption and control over the implementation of government decisions. It requires a certain level of culture of the participants, causing readiness of both the authorities and civil society structures for mutual cooperation.

As for **ineffective public participation** in anti-corruption processes, for countries that have embarked on the path of transit from totalitarianism to democracy, it is precisely due, firstly, to the authorities' disinterest in public participation in their affairs, their

18 https://ru.wikipedia.org/wiki/Коррупция
19 Mikhail Gorny. Countering Corruption. http://sudanet.ru/node/12110

desire to keep "outsiders" out of them, and, secondly, to the low level of political culture of the population, their unwillingness or lack of motivation to fight corruption.

Subjective causes of corruption include the aforementioned low political culture of the population, as well as the low quality of training of civil servants.

Corruption occurs only in situations where people begin to put their own interests above public interests, and this is an important subjective reason for the spread of corruption. The sharp turn in the post-Soviet space towards the values and ideology of liberal individualism cultivated in the West has led to a shift in the socio-psychological attitudes of many people, for whom money has become the main value and corruption the main means of enrichment.

This shift in socio-psychological attitudes is manifested in the demoralization of society, lack of awareness and organization of citizens, and public passivity against the permissiveness and arbitrariness of corrupt officials. A significant difference between declared and real values forms a "double standard" of morality and behavior among citizens. Under these conditions, money becomes the measure of everything in society, the importance of a person is determined by the size of his personal fortune regardless of the means of obtaining it, and civilized social regulators of people's behavior are devalued and broken: norms of morality, law, religion, public opinion and others.

This shift, on the one hand, is an important reason for the spread of corruption, and, on the other hand, moral degradation of society is an important negative consequence of corruption. In other words, corruption is one of the causes of the above demoralization of society.

In modern conditions, corruption is the main danger and threat to the very existence of society, destroying its economy, the apparatus of power and even the state itself, whose representatives in the person of officials, instead of solving public problems, work for themselves, solving their personal problems or the problems of individual clans. It permeates all layers of society: authorities, entrepreneurs, public organizations.

V.Y. Meytus compares corruption to a cancerous tumor eating away at the social organism. "Corruption, like a cancer, eats away at this organism, its systems of functioning, production, and defense, disrupting even the genetic elements of society, and through them the gene pool of the country in which the society exists. Moreover, having originated in one place, corruption spreads its metastases to other organs, destroying their work and poisoning the whole organism[20] ".

The spread of corruption leads to severe economic, political and social consequences.

Economic consequences of corruption: inefficient use of budget funds, price increase due to corruption costs, expansion of shadow economy, reduction of market efficiency, etc.

Corruption disrupts the mechanism of market competition, giving the advantage not to the one who is competitive, but to the one who bribed; it promotes monopolism in the economy, reduces the efficiency of its functioning and discredits the idea of free

20 Meytus V.Y. Corruption. Economic and information analysis. M., 2003. C. 6.

competition. Corrupt distribution of government contracts and allocation of loans, prevents the effective implementation of government programs.

Privatization is an important source of corruption. Significance of economic damage here is determined by the scale of privatization and weak control over its progress. Corruption violations are manifested in the misappropriation of funds, underpricing of privatized objects, manipulation of tender conditions, buying up enterprises by officials through proxies, etc. The corruption is a major source of corruption in privatization.

Corruption in the banking sector manifests itself in obtaining preferential loans, credits and credits; it leads to a decrease in tax revenues to the state budget, capital outflow abroad and hampers the ability of the state to effectively perform its economic, political and social functions.

Unfortunately, our country does not calculate the economic damage caused to society and the state by corrupt transactions. However, some idea of the scale of this damage can be obtained from data on other countries[21] .

In Russia, the level of corruption covered more than 80% of the state apparatus, and the total amount of funds raised for this purpose exceeded hundreds of billions of dollars.

In Italy, public spending on road construction fell by 20% following Operation Clean Hands, an anti-corruption operation.

According to research by Harvard University scientists, it is estimated that reducing the corruption of a country from the level of Mexico to the level of Singapore produces an effect equivalent to a 20% increase in tax collection.

The most common source of grand corruption worldwide is public contracts and procurement. For them, damage assessments (and they tend to be the most significant) have been conducted most often. According to estimates, corruption losses in this area often exceed 30% of all budget expenditures on these items.

According to Udo Miller, head of the Accounts Chamber of the State of Hesse (Germany), bribes in this area often reach 20% of the amount of the deals concluded; at the same time, the bribes are not paid in cash, but are transferred to the appropriate persons through front companies or take the form of inflated invoices for the work performed. Experts estimate that some 40 per cent of all buildings commissioned by the federal, state and municipal authorities are overcharged. According to the Chief Public Prosecutor of Frankfurt am Main, corruption in construction causes an annual loss of DM 10 billion to the state, in particular by inflating the real cost of work by 30%.

Political consequences of corruption: it contributes to the shift of policy objectives from national to clan and group goals, undermining the country's prestige in the international arena and causing its political and economic isolation (few serious foreign players will want to get involved with representatives of such clan and group interests).

---

21 See: State Policy of Counteracting Corruption and Shadow Economy in Russia. Materials of the All-Russian Scientific Conference (Moscow, June 6, 2007). - M., 2007. C. 252-254.

It is from the figures who hide their corruption capitals abroad that a "fifth column" can be formed, capable of betraying the interests of the country's national security. "Corruption reduces public confidence in the authorities, causes disappointment in the values of democracy and can contribute to the transition to another, more rigid form of state structure - dictatorship"[22] .

Social consequences: corruption causes unfair redistribution of life benefits in favor of narrow oligarchic groups, increasing property inequality among the population, impoverishment of a significant part of society and increasing social tension that threatens political stability in the country. In the public consciousness the perception of the defenselessness of citizens in the face of the authorities and crime is formed.

4. Corruption in Kazakhstan

As noted above, the problem of corruption is also relevant for modern Kazakhstan. Our country is one of the most corrupt countries in the world. In 2016, according to the international non-governmental organization Transparency International, Kazakhstan ranked 131st out of 176 countries (29 points out of 100) on the level of corruption perception.

As in other countries, grassroots corruption is the most widespread in Kazakhstan, covering the middle and lower levels of government and involving direct contacts of the population with officials. The majority of the republic's population is regularly associated with this type of corrupt relations. Very often these relations are formed at the initiative of the population: they arise when it is more profitable for a citizen to give a bribe to an official than to spend time on a trip to the bank to pay, say, a fine for a traffic violation, or to speed up the time of obtaining, for example, a permit to open a store.

But the highest damage to society and the state is caused by the highest corruption, which involves top-ranking government officials involved in the consideration of financing, lending, privatization, public procurement, banking operations, who often make decisions on multi-billion dollar public contracts for the construction of large facilities, etc.

The following examples show the scale of the highest corruption in our country: according to press reports, in 2014 the following were brought to criminal responsibility: ex-chairman of the Agency for Regulation of Natural Monopolies M. Ospanov (on suspicion of receiving a bribe of 300 thousand dollars), former head of the national company "Kazakhstan Farysh Sapary" G. Myrzakulov (sentenced to 12 years in prison on charges of receiving a bribe of 272 thousand dollars and more than 75 million tenge). Myrzakulov (sentenced to 12 years in prison on charges of receiving a bribe of 272 thousand dollars and more than 75 million tenge), Deputy Minister of Defense General B. Maikeev (sentenced to six years in prison on charges of receiving a bribe of about 1 million 500 thousand dollars), former Vice Minister of Agriculture M. Umiryaev (sentenced to 10 years in prison on charges of receiving a large bribe

---

22 Malikova A. Sh. Causes and conditions contributing to the emergence of corruption. sapanet.ru/Kafedra/Podrazd/malikov.doc

from a businessman). These examples can be continued.

The entrenched nature of corruption in Kazakhstan and the difficulty of combating it is evidenced by the following fact. According to the Republican Anti-Corruption Program for 2011-2015 approved by the government, by 2015 Kazakhstan was supposed to reach the 90th place in the Transparency International rating by the Corruption Perception Index. However, as noted above, by 2015 it was still in 140th place.

The rapid spread of corruption in Kazakhstan, as well as in other republics of the former Soviet Union, emerges from the late 1980s, when denationalization of the economy began on the basis of adopted laws on state enterprises and leases, on cooperation, etc., and especially from the early 1990s, when privatization of state enterprises began, in which representatives of the former Soviet bureaucratic apparatus, high-ranking party functionaries, their relatives and acquaintances took an active part. "Having initial capital in the form of personal connections, financial resources and management levers, they created cooperatives, centers for scientific and technical cooperation of youth.... About 10% of commercial structures in the late 80s and early 90s were established by the Party and Komsomol nomenclature."[23] .

It is in this period that the criminal corrupt link between business and government is laid, blurring the boundary between private and public interests and beginning to spread corrupt consciousness not only among the authorities, but also among business and society as a whole.

According to experts, the highest level of corruption in modern Kazakhstan is observed in the customs structure and judicial system. As noted by the former State Secretary of Kazakhstan M. Kul-Mukhamed, "despite repeated harsh warnings of the head of our state, the level of corruption in the country is decreasing very slowly. Customs authorities cause special complaints in this matter. It is here that a corrupt environment has formed, which can be called a whole industry. With Kazakhstan's accession to the Customs Union, this trend is becoming particularly relevant. Therefore, all issues related to it should be under strict state control"[24] .

Smuggling techniques have become widespread in Kazakhstan, when goods are registered at border crossings as imported under the "temporary import regime", for which no excise duty is imposed. But instead of being exported from the country, these goods are sold on the domestic market. Identical schemes are used in post-Soviet states to export goods supposedly "duty free" which are then sold to consumers in the domestic market.

The scale and trends in the spread of corruption in our country are evidenced by the following facts: if in 2012, 1,659,000 corruption offenses were detected in Kazakhstan, then only in the first seven months of 2015. - 1,728,000 (hereinafter figures are taken from the article by D. Satpayev "Corruption in Kazakhstan and the quality of public

---

23 S.P.Peregudov, N.Y.Lapina, I.S.Semenenko. Interest Groups in the Russian State. - Moscow: Editorial UrsS, 1999. C.68.

24 Cited from: http://www.ide.go.jp/Japanese/Publish/Download/Report/2012/pdf/C24_ch3.pdf

administration". http://www.ide.go.jp/Japanese/Publish/Download/Report/2012/pdf/C24_ch3.pdf). Shadow turnover in Kazakhstan exceeds $30 billion dollars a year, of which part of the money is spent on corrupt services; about 20% of companies pay bribes to officials. The scale of the "shadow" economy is at least 20% of the gross domestic product, and according to some experts, this figure reaches 40%. And, according to some experts, as soon as the level of the "shadow" economy passes 33% of GDP, and more than 40% of the population is employed there, the economy no longer responds to regulatory measures from the state and there is a serious threat to the national security of the country as a whole.

Every year, public procurement accounts for 15-20% of the total number of identified corruption offenses.

In addition to public procurement, corruption is very widespread in the areas of licensing and permit system and implementation of control and supervisory functions.

The wide scope of the "shadow" economy in the country is associated with the presence of informal centers of power, which are a kind of symbiosis between corrupt officials and organized crime.

The colossal scale of the "shadow" economy has caused a wide outflow of financial resources from the country. According to some data, over the past 20 years, about 138 billion dollars have been taken out of the country to offshore.

All these phenomena cannot but have a negative impact on the legal culture of the population and cause serious distortions in the value orientations of the population, leading to "criminalization of consciousness" of a significant number of citizens. The scale of spread of "criminalization of consciousness" of citizens of Kazakhstan can be judged by the following fact[25] . In the city of Semey, a police captain organized "recruitment" for bribes of employees of the mythical "Top Secret Directorate (SSD) of the KNB RK" out of self-serving fraudulent motives. Over several months, hundreds of people (!), having given the fraudster a total of 22 million tenge in bribes, tried to get a place in this non-existent structure. As noted by Kazakhstani economist K. Berentaev, "...a 'system of values of a corrupt person' has been formed in Kazakhstan, corruption has become the norm, it is not considered immoral. In the economic sphere, instead of competition in the quality of goods and services, there is "competition in the market of bribes"[26] .

Corrupt relations have also penetrated deeply into the system of selection of personnel for responsible government positions: there are more and more cases when during the selection process the priority is given not to the candidate's professionalism and high moral qualities, but to personal loyalty and nepotism, as well as to the one who will give a big bribe.

Such an approach leads to paralysis of power at all levels, because an official who has

---

25 See: T. Kuchukov. Casting national security, or the Extraordinary Adventures of Captain Tukenova / Vremya, 22.10.2015. C. 6.

26 Cited from: Amina Jalilova. Round table "Corruption in the Republic of Kazakhstan: security in danger". 16.05.2012. Source: http://panoramakz.com/archiv/2011/30.htm

spent on a bribe, who has taken his post, thinks more about how to return and multiply the money spent, rather than about the cause.

In recent years in Kazakhstan at the local level, the practice of creating territorial funds under almost every akimat has spread, to which business representatives are supposed to make "voluntary" contributions, which, according to the authors of this idea, go "to help orphans, low-income families, improvement of public areas, etc.". In fact, these funds create a breeding ground for corruption, as they are spent uncontrollably.

As can be seen from the above, corruption in our country has taken deep roots, it has penetrated into all pores of the social organism and poses a threat to the state security of the Republic of Kazakhstan.

TOPIC 2. INTERNATIONAL EXPERIENCE IN IMPLEMENTING ANTI-CORRUPTION POLICIES

Plan

1. Corruption in the history of world culture.
2. International legal means of combating corruption.
3. Experience of anti-corruption efforts in selected countries.

1. Corruption in the history of world culture

Corruption as a social phenomenon has been known since antiquity and it probably originated from the custom of making gifts, and it emerged much earlier than the emergence of the state. With the emergence of the state and in the process of its development and complexity, with the emergence of a layer of professional officials, it becomes widespread. In the extant literary monuments of Egypt, Mesopotamia, Judea, India and China - in all centers of ancient Eastern civilizations - there is information about attempts to combat this phenomenon. In the Indian treatise of the 4th century BC. "Arthashastra" notes that "the property of the king cannot be, even in a small way, not misappropriated by those in charge of this property". It lists 40 ways of embezzling state property and draws the disappointing conclusion that it is easier to guess the path of birds in the sky than the tricks of cunning officials.

In the literary monuments of ancient Egypt, where a huge bureaucratic apparatus of officials was formed, creating lawlessness and arbitrariness towards ordinary people, special attention was paid to the venality of judges, often deciding court disputes in favor of those who gave a larger bribe.

It is not by chance that ancient monuments first of all speak about corruption of judges. We also find condemnation of corruption in the sacred texts of Christianity and Islam. "Thou shalt not take gifts; for gifts make the blind blind to see, and turn the cause of the upright" (Bible, Exod. 23:8). "Do not misappropriate one another's property unlawfully, nor bribe judges to deliberately appropriate some of the property of others" (Qur'an 2:188).

Already in Ancient Rome the term "corruption" began to be used in the meanings: "to change testimony in court for money" and "to bribe a judge": "Would you consider it a harsh decree of law to punish with death the judge or mediator who was appointed at the trial [to try the case] and was found to have accepted a gratuity in [the] case?"[27] .

As we can see, the history of corruption is as old as the history of human civilization known to us, wherever it took place: in Egypt, Rome or Judea. Vindictiveness is mentioned in Russian chronicles of the XIII century. The first legislative restriction of corrupt practices belongs to Ivan III. And under Ivan the Terrible, the death penalty was first introduced as a punishment for excessive bribery.

For a long time corruption was viewed mainly from an ethical point of view, as a moral

[27] Textbook on the history of state and law of foreign countries / ed. by V. A. Tomsinov. A. Tomsinov. - Moscow: Zertsalo, 1999. C. 120.

problem, an inevitable evil caused by the existing morality, and only since the end of the 18th century in the West there has been a breakthrough in society's attitude towards this phenomenon.

The influence of the ideas of the great French enlighteners gradually formed the idea that state power exists for the citizens, for their benefit; it is created and maintained by the subjects in exchange for honest, selfless service of officials to their interests. And already in the world's first state document based on the ideas of these thinkers, the U.S. Constitution of 1787, the Constitution of the United States emphasizes that "on account of treason, the Constitution of the United States of America. - It is emphasized that "on account of treason, bribery, or any other high crime or misdemeanor punishable by law" (Article 11.4), the President may be impeached (removed from power) by the U.S. Congress.

In the most democratically developed countries in the 19th and 20th centuries, society began to exert more and more influence on the quality of work of the state apparatus, which led to a decrease in the level of corruption in these countries compared to other countries. This is despite the strengthening of political parties and state regulation in these countries, which led to a new type of corruption - collusion between the political elite and big business.

During this period, large private business develops, which in the conditions of strengthening state regulation and the power of officials begins to resort to "state capture" - to the direct subordination of the activities of politicians and top officials to the cause of protecting the interests of capital.

The growing influence of political parties after the Second World War in Western countries gave rise to the so-called political corruption, the essence of which is that large firms and transnational corporations pay not personally to politicians, but to party coffers for lobbying their interests.

In the second half of the 20th century, corruption entered the international arena: bribery of top officials of many countries by transnational corporations became widespread. A classic example is the scandal with the American firm Lockheed, which in the 1970s paid large bribes to high-ranking politicians and officials in Germany, Japan and other countries to sell their airplanes. Around this time, corruption began to be recognized as one of the global problems of our time, hindering the development of all countries in the world.

Often there was a paradoxical situation when one and the same person simultaneously held important positions in both the state and commercial sectors of the economy; as a result, many officials abused their position, not even accepting bribes, but directly protecting their personal interests.

In the 1990s, bribery of government officials became widespread in the former republics of the Soviet Union, including Kazakhstan.

2. International legal tools against corruption

The first state to adopt anti-corruption legislation was the USA. As early as 1977, the

Foreign Corrupt Practices Act was adopted here. Following the USA, anti-corruption legislation was developed in other countries that recognized the danger of corruption for their political and economic development. More and more politicians are beginning to realize that only the efforts of the international community can counter this evil. Moreover, the international fight against corruption should not only be a system of relations on anti-corruption issues between states represented by their bodies, but also between international governmental and non-governmental organizations, transnational corporations, financial bodies and other organizations. This system should include coordinated anti-corruption policies, strategies and tactics, the development of international agreements and treaties, and their incorporation into the domestic legislation of states.

The adoption of legislation on corruption in many countries has allowed the accumulation of certain experience in combating this evil and made it possible to identify the necessary stages in the organization of this work, the main of which are[28] :

1. Recognition by the state and citizens of the country of the problem of corruption as a threat to national security;

2. Distinguishing between the internal and external, political and economic aspects of the threat;

3. Formation of stable and effective anti-corruption legislation, taking into account the experience of other states;

See: http://edu53.ru/np-includes/upload/2012/07/13/2631.pdf

4. Establishment of an effective anti-corruption mechanism, including an independent judiciary;

5. Cultivating an atmosphere of intolerance and complete rejection of corrupt behavior of individual members and social groups in society.

This experience has led to a very important conclusion: corruption can only be defeated by uniting the efforts of government agencies, civil society and the international community as a whole.

And one more conclusion from the experience of the national fight against corruption: defeating it requires[29] :

1. Strong political will of the countries' leadership and a unified state policy against corruption;

2. Permanent social control by civil society over the entire system of public administration;

3. Strict accountability of those in authority to truly independent bodies, which in turn have the power to hold those individuals to account, regardless of the height of their social status.

---

[28] See: http://edu53.ru/np-includes/upload/2012/07/13/2631.pdf

29 See: http://edu53.ru/np-includes/upload/2012/07/13/2631.pdf

Finally, the analysis of the experience of individual countries has shown that "all other things being equal, anti-corruption achievements are more visible where historical traditions, national mentality, religious experience and other spiritual and moral factors ensure the formation in the public consciousness of the idea of an official as a respected person. A person whose task is state defense and protection of the rights and interests of citizens"[30] .

Globalization, which is becoming more and more widespread in the world, has led to the fact that corruption has become an increasingly negative influence on the development of most countries, moreover, it is becoming transnational in nature. This circumstance could not but prompt the international community to strive to develop international means of combating this phenomenon. The international community was faced with the task of developing an international anti-corruption strategy, which would represent a set of legal, political, organizational 3 measures aimed at[31] :

- formation of anti-corruption attitudes in society;
- raising awareness of the harms of corruption;
- ensuring international standards of qualification of corruption offenses, unification of jurisdictional parameters;

Creating an atmosphere of transparency, primarily in the financial sphere, to ensure the possibility of detecting corrupt acts;

- observance of the principle of inevitability of punishment;
- Ensuring fair compensation for damages from corruption offenses to the affected entities.

Since the 1970s, the problem of corruption has been on the agenda of various international forums. Thus, in the materials of the Vth UN Congress on the Prevention of Crime and the Treatment of Offenders (1975) for the first time corruption is referred to one of the types of dangerous crimes, and in the Resolution of the VIII UN Congress (1990) it is referred to global problems that threaten all mankind.

A number of instruments have been adopted specifically to combat corruption: the resolution on "Corruption in Public Administration" (1990), the declaration on "Combating Corruption and Bribery in International Business Transactions" (1996), the "International Code of Conduct for Public Officials" (1996), the "Global Programme against Corruption" (1999) and the "Convention against Transnational Organized Crime" (2000). These instruments define the concept of criminalized corruption and provide guidance to States on criminalizing acts of corruption and developing measures to prevent and detect corruption among public officials in order to ensure that corruption is effectively combated on the basis of common standards.

In October 2003, the "UN Convention against Corruption" was adopted as a **binding** instrument for all states that have ratified it.

30 http://edu53.ru/np-includes/upload/2012/07/13/2631 .pdf

[31] См.: http://www.law.edu.ru/doc/document.asp?docID=1222884&subID=100087759, 100087761

In order to draw the attention of the world community to the problem of corruption, the United Nations established the International Day against Corruption on December 9.

In 1995, Transparency International (Transparency International, meaning "Transparency International"), a non-profit, independent organization for the study and fight against corruption, was established. The organization's main goal is to create an anti-corruption environment that prevents the existence and spread of corruption. In order to achieve this goal, TI publishes annual reports containing the CPI (Corruption Perception Index) data for most countries in the world in order to create an anti-corruption attitude in society and an atmosphere of intolerance towards corruption.

At present, the main international document on combating corruption, which most countries are guided by, is the UN Convention against Corruption, ratified by the Republic of Kazakhstan in May 2008. This document, developed against the background of growing concern of the world community about the scale of development and claims of corruption, defines the following objectives[32] :

- Promoting the adoption and strengthening of measures aimed at preventing and combating corruption more effectively and efficiently;

- Promote, facilitate and support international cooperation and technical assistance in preventing and combating corruption, including asset recovery;

- Promoting integrity, accountability and the proper management of public affairs and public property (chap. 1, art. 1).

The Convention also outlines the scope of application of[33] - in the prevention, investigation and prosecution of corruption and the suspension of transactions (freezing), seizure, confiscation and return of proceeds of crime established in accordance with this convention (Ch. 1, Art. 3).

It is not necessary, the Convention notes, that harm or damage be caused to State property in the commission of the offense, but rather that the act of corruption be manifest.

A long period of preparation preceded the adoption of the Convention. In the period from 1996 to 1999, a number of international regional organizations prepared and adopted documents related to the Convention. Among them are the African Union, the European Union, the League of Arab States, the Organization of American States, the Organization for Economic Cooperation and Development, the Council of Europe, the Council for Customs Cooperation and others.

The Preamble of the Convention emphasizes that the problems caused by the international spread of corruption constitute threats to the stability and security of societies, undermine the principles of democracy; they are in conflict with democratic and ethical values, contradict the ideas of justice and are detrimental to sustainable development and the rule of law.

---

[32] See: http://articlekz.com/article/6958

33 See: http://articlekz.com/article/6958

Corruption, it says here, has done enormous damage to sustainable development, recognized by the international community as the basis for overcoming poverty, underdevelopment and inequality both within and between countries. It has struck first and foremost those countries where sustainable development is needed first and foremost, shattering the expectations of the population. Representatives of the international community are "concerned about ... by cases of corruption involving large amounts of assets, which can represent a significant proportion of the resources of States, and which jeopardize the political stability and sustainable development of those States"[34] .

Representatives of the international community, the Preamble notes, "are convinced that corruption is no longer a localized problem but has become a transnational phenomenon that affects the societies and economies of all countries, making international cooperation in preventing and combating corruption essential"[35] .

This is why the UN Convention proposes a broad and effective coordination of efforts to reduce the level of corruption offenses both in individual countries and in the global community as a whole. Among the forms of cooperation, various options are envisaged - from technical assistance to mutual legal assistance of states. Measures include the return of bank assets to the country of origin if their corrupt nature is established.

An important place in anti-corruption policy is given to civil society institutions and various non-governmental organizations, which should be encouraged and conditions should be created for their access to the relevant anti-corruption bodies, otherwise respecting the anonymity of personalities.

In addition to defining the concept of "corruption" itself, the Convention provides almost the entire list of types of corruption offenses, the main ones being[36] :

- Bribery of public national officials;
- bribery of members of state representative bodies;
- bribing foreign political figures;
- bribery in the private sector;
- Bribery of officials of international organizations;
- bribing judges;
- use of official position for personal gain;
- laundering money derived from acquisitive crimes.

The penalties for all these offenses, the document emphasizes, should be adapted to the national laws of each country party to the Convention.

A special place in the Convention is given to the problems of international cooperation

---

34 State Policy of Counteraction to Corruption and Shadow Economy in Russia / Materials of the All-Russian Scientific Conference (Moscow, June 6, 2007) - M., Scientific Expert, 2007. C. 271-272.

35 Cited in: State policy of counteraction to corruption ... C. 274.

36 See: http://edu53.ru/np-includes/upload/2012/07/13/2631.pdf

and mutual legal assistance for the recovery of assets stolen and transferred outside the State in the course of acts of corruption.

The Convention challenges States parties to establish a national legislative framework against corruption. This framework should be quite extensive and include all possible acts of corruption.

At the regional level, anti-corruption legislation is supplemented by documents of the Council of Europe, the European Union, the Organization of American States, the Commonwealth of Independent States and others. For example, the Criminal Law Convention on Combating Corruption of the European Community (1999), the Organization for Economic Cooperation and Development Convention on Combating Bribery of Foreign Public Officials in International Business Transactions (1999) and others.

3 Anti-Corruption Experiences in Selected Countries

The diversity of forms and types of corruption gives rise to a variety of ways of combating it: from prosecuting those found guilty of corruption and removing them from their positions, sentencing them to fines and imprisonment in some countries, to executing such criminals in others (e.g. China).

In a comparative analysis of corruption in the world, all countries are conditionally divided into two large groups - those in which the fight against corruption yields significant results, and countries with virtually zero results of this fight.

The study of anti-corruption programs implemented in countries that have achieved significant success in this fight is of great practical importance for the use of their experience in countries with poor results, which includes Kazakhstan (CPI - 29 points out of 100).

The least corrupt countries in the top 20 in the corruption ranking that have formed an anti-corruption strategy at the state level are, in descending order: Denmark, New Zealand, Finland, Sweden, Switzerland, Norway, Singapore, the Netherlands, Canada, Germany, Luxembourg, the United Kingdom, Australia, Iceland, Belgium, Hong Kong, Austria, the United States, Ireland[37] .

Governments in these countries recognize corruption as a serious national security issue and view it as an external and internal threat. Therefore, efforts to curb corruption in these countries are extensive and, as a rule, institutionalized, i.e., they have established special anti-corruption bodies and programmes.

Let us consider the peculiarities of anti-corruption fight in some of them.

The **United States of America** (18th most corrupt) was among the first to develop and implement a comprehensive anti-corruption strategy, the main areas of which are[38] :

- economic reform aimed at loosening government regulation;

[37] See: http://www.transparency.org/cpi2014/results
38 http://edu53.ru/np-includes/upload/2012/07/13/2631.pdf

- increasing the openness of administrative processes;
- restructuring the activities of the state apparatus, reducing bureaucratic structures and reducing their influence on the economy;
- Improving the functioning of the courts;
- reforming commercial legislation, especially on the problems of the securities market, real estate, intellectual property, and ecology;
- Strengthening civil society and enhancing independent media;
- eradication of internal corruption in law enforcement agencies.

The United States has an anti-corruption legal and regulatory framework developed in the 1970s and 1990s, on the basis of which, in addition to state bodies to combat crime in general (e.g., the FBI), bodies specializing only in acts of corruption have been established. For example, the U.S. Department of Justice has a special department to control the official behavior of elected and appointed officials, investigate crimes during election campaigns, and enforce ethics laws by government officials.

U.S. anti-corruption agencies strictly monitor officials' compliance with the prohibition to hold any paid position outside the civil service, to use official information for personal gain, to receive gifts and gratuities. For receiving illegal remuneration, an official is necessarily dismissed from service with disqualification from holding a position in a government agency. Any high-ranking civil servant, after resignation, is not entitled to represent anyone's interests before the agency in which he or she served. In order to avoid interference of interested structures in the investigation of criminal cases against top officials, the U.S. legislation provides for a special procedure for appointing a prosecutor to lead the case - this is carried out by a special division of the District Federal Court in Washington.

Committees of the U.S. Congress have broad powers to investigate corruption cases - they have the authority to investigate offenses committed by the president and the highest officials of the country.

Unlike many countries, including Kazakhstan, where criminal liability is incurred only when a bribe is received by an official, U.S. law criminalizes the **offer, promise** and giving of a bribe in exchange for the commission of illegal acts by an official[39] .

It also criminalizes an official who "directly or indirectly demands as a bribe, solicits, receives, accepts or agrees to receive or accept anything of value personally or for any other person or organization"[40] in return for any unlawful act or omission in office. This wording shows that it is not necessary that the bribe be paid in favor of the official; it may be given to another person specified by the official or to a certain political party, i.e., liability is incurred even if self-interest is not proven. Kazakhstani legislation does not punish a bribe given to a party or other organization indicated by an official acting in the interests of the bribe-giver, unless it has become the official's personal property.

39 http://www4.law.cornell.edu/uscode/18/201.html
40 Ibid.

The desire of the United States to eliminate by law not only possible acts of corruption, but also any conditions conducive to the spread of this phenomenon, is evidenced by the fact that there is a penalty for stimulating lawful actions of officials, for example, for speeding up the passage of documents for obtaining a permit (giving so-called "tips"). In the U.S., an official is entitled to receive remuneration for his work only from the government. It is believed that the receipt of so-called "tips" destroys the system of government administration and creates a desire of officials to receive such tips from everyone who asks for their help[41] .

The so-called "general bribery", when an official receives remuneration from individuals or organizations without any connection to his or her action or inaction, is also a criminal offense in the United States. In Kazakhstan, such actions are not considered bribery, and until the connection between the receipt of money and a particular action in favor of the bribe-giver is proved, the official cannot be held criminally liable.

The fight against corruption is made easier by the fact that there are virtually no "untouchables" in the United States: there are no immunities that allow officials to avoid punishment for corrupt behavior. Any official, including the president of the country, can be held criminally liable once they have been removed from office.

As is well known, the post-Soviet mentality of citizens of the former Soviet Union republics has developed a stable stereotype of negative attitude towards those who try to report to the competent authorities about the facts of law violation, including corruption ("sexots", "Pavlik Morozovs", "snitches"), which undoubtedly complicates the anti-corruption fight. In the United States of America, such acts are encouraged and a whistleblower protection law has been adopted to encourage citizens to report corruption to the competent authorities. Under this law, an official who prosecutes a subordinate for reporting wrongdoing in an organization is subject to disciplinary action on the initiative of the Special Council investigating the prosecution.

The United States was the first country in the world to adopt a law prohibiting bribery of foreign officials in the course of business (the Foreign Corrupt Practices Act, passed in 1977), extending its jurisdiction over corruption cases beyond its borders. One of the most recent examples of the application of this law is the initiation of a corruption case against FIFA President J. Blatter in 2015.

The **Netherlands** (8th most corrupt country) has developed and implemented an anti-corruption system, the main areas of which are[42] :

- a system of monitoring of possible points of corruption in state and public organizations, and strict control over the activities of persons at these points;

- a system for selecting persons for positions that are dangerous from the point of view of corruption;

41 See: Nikiforov B.S., Reshetnikov F.M. Modern American Criminal Law. M.: Nauka, 1990. C. 159.
42 See: INDEM Foundation. Russia and Corruption: Who's Who? International experience in the fight against corruption: from China's failures to Israel's successes // Clean Hands. 1999. № 3. C. 12-13.

- a system of penalties for corrupt practices, with the main measure being the prohibition to work in state organizations and the loss of all social benefits provided by the civil service;

- a system of incentives for positive actions of officials, aimed at making it financially and morally beneficial for the official to behave honestly and effectively;

- a state security system to combat corruption of the type of special police with significant powers to detect cases of corruption has been established.

Specialized and journalistic literature emphasizes the impressive success of **Singapore's** anti-corruption policy (the 7th most corrupt country in the world). Its central link is a permanent specialized anti-corruption body - the Corruption Investigation Bureau, which has political and

functional autonomy[43] . This independent body investigates and seeks to prevent corruption in the public and private sectors of Singapore's economy, with the Prevention of Corruption Act accurately characterizing corruption in terms of various forms of "remuneration". The Bureau probes cases of malpractices among public officials and reports them to the relevant authorities for necessary disciplinary action. The Bureau examines the modus operandi of potentially corruption-prone public bodies to detect possible weaknesses in governance. If it is found that such gaps may lead to corruption and abuse, the Bureau recommends appropriate action to the heads of these departments.

The main thrust of Singapore's anti-corruption policy is to "seek to minimize or eliminate the conditions that create both the incentive and the opportunity to induce an individual to commit corrupt acts"[44] .

An important factor in the successful fight against corruption in these countries has been the formation of a kind of "culture of transparency", which is based on openness of information, freedom of the press, and the participation of civil society in monitoring the activities of the state. The use of new Internet technologies to achieve transparency, provide information, and involve the public in the anti-corruption fight has become common practice in these countries.

---

43 See: Mark Hong. Singapore - the country that defeated corruption. http://world.ng.ru/ azimuth/2000-05-18/6_sing.html

44 Organized crime: trends, prospects of struggle. - Vladivostok, 1999. C. 253.

TOPIC 3. ESSENCE AND STRUCTURE OF ANTI-CORRUPTION POLICY IN KAZAKHSTAN

Plan

1. "UN Global Program against Corruption" as a methodological basis for the anti-corruption strategy of the Republic of Kazakhstan.
2. Anti-Corruption Strategy of the Republic of Kazakhstan for 2015-2025.

1. "UN Global Program against Corruption as a methodological basis for the anti-corruption strategy of the Republic of Kazakhstan

Article 1.8) of the Law of the Republic of Kazakhstan "On Combating Corruption" defines **anti-corruption** policy as "a state policy based on legal and organizational measures and aimed at combating corruption, as well as increasing public confidence in the activities of state bodies".

Analysis of the situation in Kazakhstan allows us to conclude that here, as in most republics of the former Soviet Union, minimizing corruption in the short term is unrealistic, so today only the task of limiting the scale of corruption is set.

As it is emphasized in many UN documents, it is impossible to successfully develop along the path of progress without solving this problem. Corruption hinders the stable development of society and undermines its security. It impedes effective governance and economic growth, nullifies the value of democracy. Corruption in business eliminates fair competition and contributes to the growth of monopolization of all spheres of the economy.

Successful anti-corruption efforts, it notes, can only be achieved through joint action by States themselves, civil society and the international community as a whole. The following principles should underpin the strategy for such joint action:

- strong political will of the countries' leadership and a unified state policy against corruption;
- constant social control by civil society over the entire system of public administration;
- strict accountability of those in authority to truly independent bodies, which in turn have the power to hold these individuals accountable regardless of their social status.

The UN Global Programme against Corruption, developed and adopted by the UN, is devoted to the concretization and expansion of these principles, supplemented by two documents: "Anti-Corruption Toolkit and the UN Guide to Anti-Corruption Policies, which are part of the Program. According to the intention of the drafters, this Program should help states to develop national anti-corruption strategies, i.e. it should serve as a methodological basis for anti-corruption efforts in all countries.

The main recommendations of the UN Program are summarized as follows.

1. It is necessary to create an independent anti-corruption commission, including

representatives of both government and public structures, including opposition ones. Its purpose is to develop a state anti-corruption strategy and draft anti-corruption laws.

In Kazakhstan, a State Commission on Combating Corruption with the above functions has been established by Presidential Decree.

The Program also recommends the creation of independent parliamentary commissions to investigate individual cases of corruption by the country's top officials, which has not yet been established in Kazakhstan.

2. It is suggested that each country should adopt its own anti-corruption program, providing for the development of anti-corruption legislation.

Today, Kazakhstan has an "Anti-Corruption Strategy of the Republic of Kazakhstan for 2015-2025".

While giving anti-corruption legislation an important role, at the same time, the UN Program prioritizes not punitive, but preventive measures, prevention of corruption, in which civil society structures and, first of all, mass media should play a decisive role.

With regard to the media, Kazakhstan still has much to do to ensure that the media can take the place in the fight against corruption that the UN Program assigns to them.

The program contains a number of proposals to ensure accountability and transparency of the activities of the power structures, organization of their service on the basis of the law. In Kazakhstan, with its undeveloped democratic traditions, as repeatedly mentioned by President Nazarbayev, the task of transition from service to specific individuals to service for the benefit of society is to be solved. The solution of this task is connected, in particular, with the problem of personnel training and their career advancement. Here it is recommended to create special personnel agencies that would be engaged in selection of personnel for public service on the basis of open competition, including passing examinations on knowledge of law, which would allow replacing the system of favoritism with the system of meritocracy.

It should be noted that a lot has already been done in this direction in Kazakhstan, which will be discussed in subsequent lectures. And the task is to ensure that the principles declared in the adopted documents are implemented in the practice of today.

The program also proposes the implementation of measures to control the income of civil servants, which is still formally implemented in Kazakhstan. The UN proposes confiscation of property and income, the origin of which the official is unable or unwilling to explain, which is also not done in Kazakhstan.

The program proposes to introduce into national legislation the norms of the "International Code of Conduct for Public Officials", including in the codes of conduct of public and municipal (in Kazakhstan these are local authorities) employees the principles of impartiality, fairness, honesty, diligence, transparency, accountability in the use of entrusted resources.

The "Anti-Corruption Toolkit", which, as noted above, is a part of the UN Program, proposes that national codes of conduct for officials should provide for sanctions for violation of their norms, as well as legal liability of the heads of government bodies and public institutions for failure to enforce these norms by their subordinates. These codes should be adopted for each specific group of employees and officials (members of parliament, members of government, civil servants, police, court and prosecutors). They should provide for citizen participation in monitoring the implementation of the code of conduct by employees (e.g., through a complaints system).

The UN Program emphasizes the need to simplify administrative decision-making procedures. They should be understandable to citizens and made on the basis of clear criteria. The instructions on the basis of which decisions are made should be accessible to citizens.

An important place in the Program is given to the issue of openness in the adoption of budgets and the possibility of public control over their implementation. It is emphasized that it is necessary to develop norms obliging representative bodies to make public the draft budgets they consider and to hold public hearings on these drafts.

The UN Program attaches special importance to ensuring transparency in the distribution of state and municipal orders. As it is known, in Kazakhstan the current legislation does not fulfill this task. A significant number of orders are distributed without competitive bidding. Tenders are often of a formal nature with the result known in advance.

The definition of corruption in the UN Global Program against Corruption even includes "promising and offering a bribe" as an offense. "The Anti-Corruption Toolkit proposes that bribery should be defined as an act in which benefits are transferred not only to the official himself, but also to other persons to whom he points. For example, it may be a party to which he or she belongs or a commercial organization in the successful operation of which he or she is interested.

The Global Program recommends that countries criminalize companies that are "blind to the fact that their employees are involved in corruption, money laundering or other economic and financial crimes" and encourages countries to confiscate the proceeds of corruption. In Kazakhstan, when a specific bribe is exposed, the perpetrators are held liable, and the companies with whose consent and in whose interests they acted are not held criminally or administratively liable.

In the Criminal Code of the Republic of Kazakhstan, as recommended by the Global Program, corruption offenses are allocated to a special group (Chapter 15. Corruption and other criminal offenses against the interests of public service and public administration), which makes it possible to talk about recidivism for committing this type of acts, and about the application of additional losses of rights to persons who have committed corruption offenses.

"The UN Global Anti-Corruption Program identifies such a corruption offense as **conflict of interest.** It consists in the fact that a public official takes part in the resolution of a matter with a personal financial interest in a certain result. The UN Program proposes to qualify such actions of officials and employees as unlawful receipt of an allowance, benefit or reward, which is not a bribe, but nevertheless should be qualified as a crime.

Summing up, it should be noted that Kazakhstan has done a lot to implement the recommendations of the UN Global Anti-Corruption Program, but there is still much to be done both in the field of national legislation and in the spheres of economic, social and spiritual life of the country.

2 Anti-Corruption Strategy of the Republic of Kazakhstan for 2015-2025

Since the beginning of Kazakhstan's formation as an independent sovereign state, the problem of corruption has been regarded as one of the most important problems threatening the stable progressive development of the entire society. Therefore, in the activities of state bodies, much attention is paid to combating this phenomenon, and the first step here, of course, is the development and implementation of a regulatory framework that would underpin the legislative basis and regulate this complex and difficult work.

In line with this task, a number of anti-corruption laws have been adopted, which will be discussed in the following lectures, "a number of program documents are being implemented, a special authorized body has been established, which comprehensively implements functions in the field of civil service and anti-corruption, and international cooperation in the field of anti-corruption activities is actively carried out"[45] . Kazakhstan "purposefully and gradually follows the course of creating effective institutions and mechanisms for combating corruption that meet international standards".

Modern anti-corruption activities in our country are based on the "Anti-Corruption Strategy of the Republic of Kazakhstan for 2015-2025" adopted in December 2014. The "Anti-Corruption Strategy of the Republic of Kazakhstan for 2015-2025", which we will analyze.

The first section of the Strategy "Introduction" briefly characterizes what has been done in the field of anti-corruption fight during the years of independence. It is emphasized that the country has clearly implemented the principle of meritocracy, i.e. the nomination of capable and professionally trained people to leadership positions, regardless of their social origin and property status; a civil service system has been established, including a clear delineation and definition of the functions and powers of each body and official of the State. The introduction of information technologies in the sphere of public services has reduced the direct contacts of officials with citizens, which undoubtedly minimized the conditions for corruption.

The country, as emphasized in the Introduction, is creating prerequisites for the formation of an anti-corruption culture among the population.

At the same time, the tasks set to make Kazakhstan one of the thirty most competitive countries in the world require modernization of the anti-corruption policy of the state and increasing the role of civil society institutions in its implementation, which would

45 Hereinafter citations are quoted from: Anti-Corruption Strategy of the Republic of Kazakhstan for 2015-2025. http:// anticorruption. gov. kz/rus/nac_antikorrupcionnaya_strateg/

allow to reduce corruption manifestations as much as possible. This explains the need to adopt an anti-corruption Strategy, which is a program document in the fight against corruption. At the same time, it says here, "the emphasis should be on eliminating the preconditions of corruption, rather than on fighting its consequences". In other words, the leading role in the Strategy is given to comprehensive preventive measures capable of drastically reducing the level of corruption and eradicating the causes and conditions that give rise to it in various spheres of life of the state and society.

The Introduction also notes that the basic directions defined by the Strategy should be clarified and concretized on the basis of further analysis of the real state of corruption, its causes, motivation of corrupt behavior, and a serious and objective assessment of the state of affairs in the fight against corruption.

The second section "Analysis of the Current Situation" describes positive trends in the field of anti-corruption, the strengthening and development of which will be the key to the successful implementation of the Strategy at the present stage.

Achievement of certain positive results is associated with the adoption of anti-corruption legislation, which defined the goals, objectives, basic principles and mechanism for combating this negative phenomenon. Since 2001, state anti-corruption programs have been implemented, within the framework of which specific measures have been taken to eliminate the causes and conditions of corruption. [46]In 2002, a Commission on Combating Corruption was established under the President of the Republic of Kazakhstan, which is vested with broad supervisory powers in the area of compliance by State officials with anti-corruption legislation and, in particular, with the right to "submit to the President of the Republic of Kazakhstan proposals on giving instructions, issuing relevant acts of the President of the Republic on the issues under consideration, as well as bringing to disciplinary responsibility up to and including dismissal from office of the akims of the regions, the cities of Astana and Almaty, the governors of the regions, and the chief executive officers of the Republic of Kazakhstan.

The positive trend in the anti-corruption fight is also significantly influenced by the successful implementation of the principle of inevitability of punishment: in recent years, there has been an increase in the number of cases in which officials found guilty of corruption, regardless of their positions and ranks, are held accountable to the full extent of the law. This principled approach has been implemented in the new Criminal Code (August 2015), according to which "persons who have committed corruption offenses will not be subject to the statute of limitations, there will be a ban on probation, and a lifetime ban on the right to hold public office has been introduced". Norms on confiscation of criminally obtained property and personal responsibility of managers for combating corruption have been introduced.

But in the past period, this section notes, emphasis has been placed not only on strengthening the responsibility of public servants, but also on improving their social guarantees, which undoubtedly contributes to creating conditions for them to perform

---

46 http://adilet.zan.kz/rus/docs/U020000839_#z8

their duties in a fair and just manner.

On the basis of the implementation of the provisions of the State Program for the Further Modernization of the Law Enforcement System for the Period up to 2020 and the Concept of Personnel Policy of Law Enforcement Agencies, measures are being taken to increase the level of confidence in law enforcement agencies and to develop personnel with impeccable conduct and a high level of competence.

Work is under way to increase confidence in the judicial system, improve the mechanism for the formation of the corps of judges, develop electronic court proceedings, and make them more transparent and accessible.

There have been advances in public access to information, in particular through the establishment of e-government and the creation of Internet resources of public and private entities, allowing citizens to report corruption, including through hotlines and websites of public bodies.

Conditions have been created in the country to improve the quality of public services, the number of permits and license types of activities has been sharply reduced through the elimination of administrative barriers that hinder entrepreneurial activity, which has led to a narrowing of opportunities for corrupt practices.

"The result of this work was an annual decrease in the number of violations of the terms of rendering public services (by 8.7 times compared to 2012) and complaints about the quality of their provision (by 25%), as well as an increase in the share of automated services (by more than 2 times) and services provided through population service centers (by 51%)."

There have also been positive developments in public procurement, mainly due to increased automation.

The adoption of all these measures, this section notes, "has allowed Kazakhstan to take one of the leading positions in terms of anti-corruption activities both in the Central Asian region and among the CIS countries".

While there have been some successes in the fight against corruption in Kazakhstan, the Strategy emphasizes the complexity of developing effective countermeasures, which is due to its specificity for each individual state and the difficulties associated with its changing characteristics. In determining the causes, conditions and consequences of corruption, such factors as local mentality, national and religious peculiarities, and the level of legal culture should be taken into account.

At the same time, the Strategy states, "the main conditions for effective and systematic anti-corruption efforts are recognized as accountability and public accountability of the authorities, independence and fairness of justice, clear and easy-to-apply laws, meritocracy in the state's personnel policy, transparency of state procedures and intolerance to corruption in society.

An important link in the anti-corruption system is also prevention, creation of conditions in which corrupt practices are impossible - identification and minimization of corruption **risks,** which are understood as opportunities existing in the system of state and municipal governance for the actions (inaction) of officials and ordinary employees to illegally obtain material and other benefits in the performance of their official duties. "The assessment of corruption risks, the level of their prevalence in various spheres and industries helps to identify gaps in the state, including legal and regulatory, regulation of anti-corruption activities, problems arising in the mechanisms of state and legal regulation, as well as the development of measures aimed at improving law enforcement practice in the process of anti-corruption activities".

While noting positive developments in the prevention of corruption, the Strategy, at the same time, points to the lack of transparency in making decisions affecting the most important issues of public life, the absence of proper civil control and consideration of public opinion in the activities of the state apparatus, which leads to excessive bureaucracy, administrative barriers and abuse of authority.

It also draws attention to the problem of unresolved issues of proper enforcement of the legislative potential for combating corruption, despite the ongoing qualitative update of the basic branches of national legislation. The issues of combating corruption in the private sector have not been resolved either.

The Strategy explicitly mentions the need to "take into account certain international standards adopted in anti-corruption matters".

The second section of the Strategy concludes with a characterization of the main factors contributing to corrupt practices in modern Kazakhstan. These factors are:

- imperfection of sectoral laws, which allows for double interpretation of many norms, which creates conditions for corrupt practices;
- poor transparency of power structures, closed process of elaboration and adoption of managerial decisions;
- a wide field of direct contacts of officials with the public when providing public services, which contributes to the emergence of corruption risks;
- low level of legal culture of citizens, including officials themselves, which enables unscrupulous employees to violate the law and instructions for selfish purposes;
- low level of information and educational work to create a public atmosphere of rejection of corruption;
- insufficient level of remuneration of labor of certain categories of public officials and social guarantees in the civil service.

The third section **"Goals and Objectives"** defines the goal of the Strategy - "to increase the effectiveness of the state's anti-corruption policy, to involve the entire society in the anti-corruption movement by creating an atmosphere of "zero" tolerance for any manifestations of corruption and to reduce the level of corruption in Kazakhstan".

It also formulates the tasks - "combating corruption in the civil service; introduction of the institute of public control; combating corruption in the quasi-state[47] and private sector; prevention of corruption in courts and law enforcement agencies; formation of the level of anti-corruption culture; development of international cooperation on anti-corruption issues".

The fourth section **"Key directions, main approaches and priority measures"** formulates the main directions, approaches and measures for the implementation of anti-corruption policy in the state and public spheres of our country.

In the field of public service, it is envisaged to implement measures and create conditions under which the use of official powers for selfish purposes will be unprofitable and impossible.

One of such measures will be the declaration by civil servants not only of their income, but also of their expenditures.

To reduce the level of corruption in the state apparatus, it is envisaged to further gradually increase the salaries and social benefits of officials as the financial capacity of the state expands.

In order to reduce contacts between officials and citizens, and these contacts are one of the prerequisites for corrupt practices, measures will be taken to transfer a number of state functions to the non-governmental sector - to self-regulatory organizations, as well as to expand the scope of services provided to the public in electronic format, including such services as issuing permits.

The most corrupt area of activity in the country is the public procurement system. It is here that every fourth corruption offense is committed. Here such measures are planned as fixing a single operator, introduction of automated selection of goods, improvement of procedures for acceptance of completed works and services.

The automation of procedures for the provision of public services will be extended to customs, taxation, agriculture, land relations, and banking. The list of public services provided to the population on a "one-stop-shop" basis (through the centralized offices) will also be expanded.

The Strategy identifies the principle of transparency as a key factor in combating corruption and therefore work on its implementation will be carried out on a continuous, systematic basis, including by monitoring the quality and accessibility of public services.

Another important area of corruption prevention is public control. Its implementation requires not only increased activity of civil society institutions, but also appropriate legislative regulation.

In this regard, the preparation for the adoption of the laws "On Public Control" and "On Access to Public Information" is mentioned. The first of them "will create a legal basis for holding public hearings on issues affecting the rights and interests of citizens, public examination of decisions of state bodies, for hearing reports of managers to the

47 Quasi-state sector is a term denoting an economic unit among whose shareholders there is a state, which acts as a guarantor of this unit.

public and participation of citizens in the work of collegial bodies". The second one "will consolidate the rights of recipients of public information, the procedure for its provision, accounting and use". At present, the drafts of these two laws are published for discussion.

The Strategy also defines the main directions of anti-corruption policy in the quasi-public and private sectors, where the danger of corruption is comparable to its scale in the public sector. Particular attention is paid to organizational and legal mechanisms to ensure accountability, accountability and transparency of decision-making procedures in this sector.

The document also addresses the problem of preventing corruption in the judiciary and law enforcement agencies. As in previous spheres, the main emphasis here is placed on tightening the requirements for the selection of judicial and law enforcement personnel through competitive selection mechanisms and the principle of meritocracy, increasing transparency in the work of judges and law enforcement officers, and introducing automated systems that reduce personal contacts between officials and citizens.

The next important area of corruption prevention is the formation of an anti-corruption culture among citizens. Without an anti-corruption culture among citizens," the Strategy says, "a strong immunity to corruption, its public censure is impossible to achieve the desired result. Every Kazakhstani citizen, every family should realize that the fight against corruption is a matter for the whole society".

This work should cover all segments of Kazakhstani society and be conducted on a professional basis. The mass media are important in this endeavor.

The Strategy also touches upon the problem of development of international cooperation on anti-corruption issues. Kazakhstan's accession to the UN Convention against Corruption and other documents in this area "ensures the active participation of our country in the international anti-corruption processes.

On the one hand, it creates incentives for the use of best anti-corruption practices, on the other hand, it expands opportunities for cooperation with foreign countries.

The last, fifth, section "**Monitoring and Evaluation of the Strategy Implementation"** states that "the authorized anti-corruption body will be the main body in the mechanism of implementation of the Anti-Corruption Strategy, and all state bodies, organizations and institutions, companies with state participation, political parties and other public associations and civil society in general will be involved in the implementation of the Strategy". Concretization and gradual implementation of its provisions will be ensured by the Action Plan, which will be approved by the Government in coordination with the Presidential Administration.

An important place in the implementation of the Strategy is given to monitoring and evaluation of its implementation, which should be carried out openly with the involvement of interested government bodies, the public and the media. The annual National Report, approved by the President, on the implementation of the Strategy will be published in the mass media.

As can be seen from the above analysis of the "Anti-Corruption Strategy of the Republic of Kazakhstan for 2015-2025", this document outlines the main directions, methods and ways of combating this phenomenon, and it is a matter of putting into practice on the basis of this document.

THEME 4. LEGAL FRAMEWORK FOR COMBATING CORRUPTION IN KAZAKHSTAN

Plan

1. The Law of the Republic of Kazakhstan "On Combating Corruption" and its preventive orientation.

2. Criminal and administrative liability for corrupt practices in the Republic of Kazakhstan.

1. The Law of the Republic of Kazakhstan "On Combating Corruption" and its preventive orientation

The main legal document regulating the anti-corruption fight in the Republic of Kazakhstan is the Law "On Combating Corruption" (the "Law") adopted in November 2015 and enacted as of January 1, 2016.

Corruption is defined here as "the illegal use by persons holding responsible public office, persons authorized to perform public functions, persons equivalent to persons authorized to perform public functions, officials of their official (service) powers and related opportunities in order to obtain or extract, personally or through intermediaries, property (non-property) benefits and advantages for themselves or third parties, as well as the bribery of these persons by providing bll

The Act provides the following explanation of the concepts characterizing the persons listed above[48] :

- **person holding a responsible public office** - a person holding an office .... for the direct performance of the functions of the state and the powers of state bodies, including a member of Parliament, a judge, as well as a person holding a . political public office or an administrative public office of A corps;

- **a person authorized to perform state functions** - a civil servant, a deputy of the maslikhat;

- **a person equated to persons authorized to perform state functions** - a person elected to local self-government bodies; a citizen registered as a candidate for the President of the Republic of Kazakhstan, deputies to the Parliament of the Republic of Kazakhstan or maslikhats, as well as members of an elected body of local self-government; an employee permanently or temporarily working in a local self-government body, whose salary is paid from the state budget of the Republic of Kazakhstan; a person performing managerial functions in a local self-government body; a person performing managerial functions in a local self-government body; an employee of the National Bank of the Republic of Kazakhstan and its departments; an employee of the National Bank of the Republic of Kazakhstan and its agencies; an employee of the National Bank of the Republic of Kazakhstan and its departments

48 In the following, the phrase "responsible persons" will be used instead of listing these categories of persons, unless specifically stated.

employees of the National Bank of the Republic of Kazakhstan and its departments;

- **official** - a person who permanently, temporarily or by special authority performs the functions of a representative of power or performs organizational, administrative or economic functions in state bodies, local self-government bodies, as well as in the Armed Forces of the Republic of Kazakhstan, other troops and military formations of the Republic of Kazakhstan.

The Law divides corruption offenses into two types: corruption crimes and administrative corruption offenses. The former are subject to criminal liability and punishment under the Criminal Code of the Republic of Kazakhstan, while the latter are subject to administrative liability and penalties under the Code of Administrative Offenses of the Republic of Kazakhstan.

In case of discrepancy between the Law and an international treaty ratified by the Republic of Kazakhstan, the rules of the international treaty shall apply.

The law has a pronounced preventive orientation, which is evidenced even by its title: "On Combating Corruption", as opposed to the earlier law "On Combating Corruption", as well as the basic principles of anti-corruption formulated here:

- legitimacy;
- prioritizing the protection of human and civil rights, freedoms and legitimate interests;
- of publicity and transparency;
- interaction between the state and civil society;
- systematic and comprehensive use of anti-corruption measures;
- prioritizing the application of measures to prevent corruption;
- encouraging persons who assist in combating corruption;
- inevitability of punishment for corruption offenses.

The preventive nature of the Law is also reflected in the anti-corruption objectives formulated here:

- creating an atmosphere of intolerance to corruption in society;
- identifying conditions and causes contributing to the commission of corruption offenses and eliminating their consequences;
- strengthening the interaction of anti-corruption actors;
- development of international cooperation in combating corruption;
- detection, suppression, disclosure and investigation of corruption offenses.

Another peculiarity of the Law is its openness, the possibility of further specification and clarification, bringing it in line with international legal documents on anti-corruption fight as conditions are created.

An important place in the prevention of corruption is occupied by anti-corruption monitoring, the essence of which is the collection, processing, generalization, analysis and evaluation of information related to the effectiveness of anti-corruption policies, as well as public perception and assessment of the level of corruption.

The results of such monitoring will contribute to a more thorough analysis of corruption risks and the development of effective measures to foster an anti-corruption culture. The Law defines corruption risks as "the possibility of the emergence of causes and conditions conducive to the commission of corruption offenses".

The law provides for a two-level analysis of corruption risks: external and internal. **External analysis** is carried out by the authorized anti-corruption body and is aimed at identifying corruption risks in normative legal acts and in the organizational and management activities of state bodies and organizations, subjects of the quasi-public sector. **Internal analysis** is carried out by state bodies, organizations and subjects of the quasi-public sector, based on the results of which they take measures to eliminate the causes and conditions conducive to the commission of corruption offences.

Another important area in the prevention of corruption is the formation of an anti-corruption culture, i.e. activities "to preserve and strengthen a system of values in society reflecting intolerance to corruption". This activity, the Law stresses, is carried out through a set of educational, informational and organizational measures.

The next area of corruption prevention is financial control measures that provide for the submission of declarations of income and property subject to taxation by persons holding public office and their spouses.

Failure to submit or submission of incomplete, unreliable declarations entails disciplinary responsibility in accordance with the procedure stipulated by law. Administrative responsibility is stipulated for these actions committed repeatedly.

Information on the amounts and sources of income of officials holding responsible public positions **may be** published. In other words, the Law does not require **mandatory** publication of this information.

Individuals and legal entities that participate in the performance of state property management functions shall submit reports on all property transactions and financial activities related to state property.

The measures of financial control provided for by the Law on Combating Corruption in the Republic of Kazakhstan, more than any other, come into the greatest conflict with the measures recommended by international anti-corruption documents. For example, the UN Global Program against Corruption, supplemented by two documents: "Anti-Corruption Toolkit" and "UN Guidelines on Anti-Corruption Policies", which are its constituent parts, proposes to include in the declarations not only information on income, but also on expenses, as well as to carry out confiscation of property and income, the origin of which the official is unable or unwilling to explain.

Obviously, the legislator takes into account the unpreparedness of the Kazakhstani society for such radical measures, but, at the same time, the Law clearly shows a desire to approach international standards. This is evidenced by the following provisions.

Effective January 1, 2017:

1. Expands the range of persons submitting declarations of income and property. These include:

- persons holding a responsible public office and their spouses;
- persons authorized to perform state functions and their spouses;
- officials and their spouses;
- persons equated to persons authorized to perform state functions and their spouses.

2. When acquiring property in the reporting period, these persons must indicate in their declarations the sources of covering the costs of this acquisition. As noted in the Address of the President of the Republic of Kazakhstan N.A.Nazarbayev to the people of Kazakhstan dated November 30, 2015. "Kazakhstan in the new global reality: growth, reforms, development", "From January 1, 2017, universal declaration of income and expenses will come into force. After that, measures will be taken to disclose accounts and assets, wherever they are located, to find out their origin and taxation, including with the help of the OECD".

3. Failure to submit or submission of incomplete, inaccurate declarations by these persons entails administrative liability, whereas until January 1, 2017, a norm providing only for disciplinary liability is in force.

Beginning January 1, 2020, the information reflected in the declarations filed by the following individuals and their spouses will be **subject to** publication:

- holding political public office;
- holding "A" corps administrative government positions;
- deputies of the Parliament of the Republic of Kazakhstan;
- judges of the Republic of Kazakhstan;
- persons performing managerial functions in quasi-state sector entities.

As we can see, the Law is aimed at bringing corruption prevention closer to international standards.

For preventive purposes, the Anti-Corruption Law also establishes anti-corruption restrictions to be assumed by responsible persons in order to prevent actions that may lead to the use of their powers for personal, group and other non-business interests.

Consent to the acceptance of anti-corruption restrictions by these persons shall be recorded in writing. Persons refusing to accept anti-corruption restrictions are subject to dismissal from service.

The Law defines the following anti-corruption restrictions to be undertaken by the above-mentioned persons:

- carrying out activities incompatible with the performance of public functions;

- inadmissibility of joint service (work) of close relatives, spouses and in-laws[49] ;

- use of official and other information that is not subject to official dissemination for the purpose of obtaining or extracting property and non-property benefits and advantages;

- acceptance of gifts in connection with the fulfillment of official powers in accordance with the legislation of the Republic of Kazakhstan.

The law expressly prohibits the performance of official duties if there is a conflict of interest, which is understood as "a contradiction between the personal interests of persons holding a responsible public position, persons authorized to perform public functions, persons equal to them, officials and their official powers, in which the personal interests of these persons may lead to improper performance of their official powers. In this case, they "shall be obliged to notify in writing their immediate supervisor or the management of the organization in which they work of the conflict of interest or the possibility of its occurrence as soon as they become aware of it".

The law also requires business entities to take measures to prevent corruption in the course of their activities, the main ones being:

- Establishing a system of organizational and legal mechanisms to ensure accountability, accountability and transparency of decision-making procedures;
- adherence to the principles of fair competition;
- preventing conflicts of interest;
- adopting and adhering to business ethics;
- taking measures to foster an anti-corruption culture.

The Law attaches an important importance in the prevention of corruption to the National Report on Combating Corruption, which is annually compiled by an authorized body and submitted to the President of the Republic of Kazakhstan.

The Law defines an authorized anti-corruption body as "a state body directly subordinate and accountable to the President of the Republic of Kazakhstan and its territorial subdivisions, which within the limits of its authority performs the functions of implementing the anti-corruption policy of the Republic of Kazakhstan and coordination in the field of combating corruption". [50]Although this body is not directly named in the Law itself, it is, in fact, the Agency of the Republic of Kazakhstan for Civil Service and Anti-Corruption, which carries out "leadership in the field of civil service, evaluation and control over the quality of public services, as well as, within the limits provided for by the legislation of the Republic of Kazakhstan, leadership and inter-sectoral coordination and other special executive and authorization functions for prevention, detection, suppression, disclosure and investigation of corruption. To

49 The Law defines close relatives as parents (parent), children, adoptive parents (adoptive parents), adopted children, full and half brothers and sisters, grandparents and grandchildren, and as in-laws - brothers, sisters, parents and children of a spouse.

50 Regulations on the Agency of the Republic of Kazakhstan for Civil Service and Anti-Corruption. http://tengrinews.kz/zakon/prezident_respubliki_ kazahstan/trud/id-U1400000900/

perform these functions, it has an anti-corruption service with operational and investigative powers ,

established by the Law of the Republic of Kazakhstan "On Law Enforcement Service". This Agency, according to the Law, is the first subject of anti-corruption.

The Agency for Civil Service and Anti-Corruption performs numerous functions, ranging from developing proposals to improve the legal and regulatory framework in the area of anti-corruption, identifying causes and conditions conducive to corruption, to anti-corruption education, monitoring and cooperation with civil society in this area.

In order to fulfill these functions, it is vested with the following powers:

- Requests information and materials from state bodies, organizations and officials;
- in cases of revealing violations of the legislation of the Republic of Kazakhstan on counteraction to corruption takes measures to eliminate them;
- determines the procedure for anti-corruption monitoring.

The anti-corruption service of the authorized anti-corruption body is vested with the rights of law enforcement agencies as defined by the Law of the Republic of Kazakhstan "On Law Enforcement Service".

Other anti-corruption actors are "state bodies, quasi-state actors, public associations, as well as other natural and legal persons".

The law explicitly obliges all state bodies, organizations, all quasi-public sector entities and officials to carry out anti-corruption activities. Direct detection, suppression, disclosure, investigation and prevention of corruption offenses and bringing the persons guilty of committing them to justice shall be entrusted to the bodies of prosecutor's office, national security, internal affairs, state revenues, military police, Border Service of the National Security Committee of the Republic of Kazakhstan.

The Law assigns an important place in combating corruption to the public, which is represented by individuals, public associations and other legal entities:

- reports on the facts of committing corruption offenses;
- Makes proposals to improve legislation on anti-corruption issues;
- participates in the formation of anti-corruption culture;
- interacts with other anti-corruption actors and the authorized anti-corruption body;
- conducts research, including scientific and sociological research, on anti-corruption issues;
- conducts explanatory work in the mass media and organizes socially significant events on anti-corruption issues.

As noted above, the post-Soviet mentality of citizens of the former Soviet Union republics has developed a strong stereotype of negative attitude towards those who try to report to the competent authorities about the facts of violation of the law, including corruption ("sexots", "Pavlik Morozovs", "snitches"), which undoubtedly complicates the anti-corruption fight and caused the lack of elaboration of this issue in the legislation. The United Nations Convention against Corruption proposes to encourage such acts and to encourage citizens to report facts of corruption to the competent authorities by adopting a law on whistleblower protection

This proposal of the UN Convention is reflected in the Law on Combating Corruption: Article 24 of this Law "Reporting of Corruption Offenses" explicitly obliges the competent authorities to take action on a reported corruption offense. "A person," it goes on to say, "who reports a corruption offense or otherwise assists in combating corruption shall be protected by the state and encouraged in accordance with the procedure established by the Government of the Republic of Kazakhstan".

The provisions of the UN Convention against Corruption are also reflected in the fourth chapter of the Law "Elimination of Consequences of Corruption Offenses". This section establishes, firstly, the norm and procedure for recovery (return) of illegally obtained property or the cost of illegally provided services, and, secondly, the procedure for invalidation of transactions, agreements, acts and actions committed as a result of corruption offenses.

As can be seen from the above, the Law of the Republic of Kazakhstan "On Combating Corruption" provides a broad legal framework for combating this negative phenomenon; it lays down prerequisites for further deepening and concretization of legal norms regulating this fight in accordance with the degree of economic, political, social and spiritual development of Kazakhstan society.

2. Criminal and administrative liability for corrupt practices in the Republic of Kazakhstan

As noted above, the Law "On Combating Corruption" divides corrupt practices into two types: corruption crimes and administrative corruption offenses. The former are subject to criminal liability and punishment under the Criminal Code of the Republic of Kazakhstan, while the latter are subject to administrative liability and penalties under the Code of Administrative Offenses of the Republic of Kazakhstan.

The Criminal Code of the Republic of Kazakhstan devotes a special chapter 15 to the fight against corruption: "Corruption and other criminal offenses against the interests of public service and public administration". This chapter qualifies the following types of corruption as criminal offenses subject to punishment.

1. **Abuse of official powers.** Use of official powers for the purpose of deriving benefits and advantages for oneself or other persons or organizations.

2. **Excess of power.** Committing by a person authorized to perform state functions, or a person equal to him/her, of actions that clearly exceed the limits of his/her rights and powers and entailed causing substantial harm to the rights and legitimate interests of citizens or organizations or to the legally protected interests of society or the state in order to derive benefits and advantages for himself/herself or other persons or organizations or to cause harm to other persons or organizations.

3. **Illegal participation in entrepreneurial activity.** Establishment by a person authorized to perform state functions or a person equal to him of an organization engaged in entrepreneurial activity, or participation in the management of such an organization personally or through a proxy, contrary to the prohibition established by law, if this act is associated with the provision of benefits and advantages to such an organization or with patronage in another form.

4. **Obstruction of lawful entrepreneurial activity.** Restriction of rights and legitimate interests of an individual entrepreneur or a commercial organization, restriction of their independence or other illegal interference in their activities, if these acts are committed by a person authorized to perform state functions or a person equal to him with the use of his official powers for the purpose of extracting benefits and advantages for himself or other persons or organizations.

5. **Receipt of a bribe.** Receipt by a responsible person personally or through an intermediary of a bribe in the form of money, securities, other property, right to property or benefits of a property nature for himself or other persons for actions (inaction) in favor of the briber or persons represented by him, if such actions (inaction) are within the official powers of this person, or he by virtue of his official position can facilitate such actions (inaction), as well as for general patronage or connivance.

6. **Giving a bribe** to a responsible person personally or through an intermediary.

7. **Mediation in bribery**, i.e. assisting the bribe-receiver and the bribe-giver in reaching or implementing an agreement between them to receive and give a bribe.

8. **Official forgery**, i.e. introduction of knowingly false information into official documents by a person authorized to perform state functions or a person equal to him or her, or making corrections to the said documents that distort their actual content, or issuance of knowingly false or forged documents, if these acts are committed for the purpose of deriving benefits and advantages for oneself or other persons or organizations, or causing harm to other persons or organizations.

9. **Inaction in service**, i.e. non-performance by a person authorized to perform state functions or a person equal to him of his official duties for the purpose of deriving benefits and advantages for himself or other persons or organizations, or causing harm to other persons or organizations, if this entailed a significant violation of the rights and legitimate interests of citizens or organizations or the legally protected interests of society or the state.

The Code differentiates penalties for these corruption offenses depending on the status of the offender and the gravity of the offense. Taking into account these criteria, the punishment may vary, for example, for abuse of official powers - from a fine of up to two thousand estimated monthly indices and up to eight years of imprisonment with confiscation of property, with life deprivation of the right to hold certain positions or engage in certain activities. A person authorized to perform state functions for this crime shall be punished by a fine of up to two thousand monthly calculation indices or correctional work in the same amount, or restriction of liberty for up to two years, or deprivation of liberty for the same period, with confiscation of property, with lifetime deprivation of the right to hold certain positions or engage in certain activities, and a person holding a responsible state position shall be punished by a fine of up to six thousand monthly calculation indices or correctional work in the same amount. For the same crime, which has led to grave consequences, responsible persons shall be punished by imprisonment for a term of four to eight years with confiscation of property, with lifetime deprivation of the right to hold certain positions or engage in certain activities.

The Criminal Code defines corruption offenses as other acts carried out by responsible persons using their official position in order to obtain certain advantages or property benefits. These include:

- Embezzlement or embezzlement of entrusted property;
- fraud;
- pseudo-entrepreneurship;
- Actions to issue an invoice without actual performance of work, provision of services or shipment of goods;
- creation and management of a financial (investment) pyramid scheme;
- legalization (laundering) of money and (or) other property obtained by criminal means;
- economic smuggling;
- raiding;
- organization of illegal gambling business.

The punishment for these crimes is also differentiated in relation to the category of persons responsible and the gravity of the act.

The Criminal Code classifies the following actions of military commanders and officials as corruption offenses:

- Abuse of power contrary to the interests of the service for the purpose of deriving benefits and advantages;
- abuse of power - commission by a superior or official of actions clearly beyond the limits of his rights and powers, ..., for the purpose of deriving benefits and advantages for himself or other persons or organizations or causing harm to other persons or organizations;
- inaction of authority - failure to perform official duties for the purpose of deriving benefits and advantages for oneself or other persons or organizations or causing harm to other persons or organizations, if this entailed a substantial violation of the rights and legitimate interests of citizens or organizations or the legally protected interests of society or the state,

In the Code of Administrative Offenses of the Republic of Kazakhstan, the following actions are classified as administrative corruption offenses:

- provision of illegal material remuneration by individuals to persons authorized to perform state functions or persons equated to them, illegal material remuneration, gifts, benefits or services;

- Receipt of illegal material remuneration by a person authorized to perform state functions or a person equal to him/her personally or through an intermediary of illegal material remuneration, gifts, benefits or services for actions (inaction) in favor of persons who provided them, if such actions (inaction) are within the official powers of a person authorized to perform state functions or a person equal to him/her;

- provision of illegal material remuneration by legal entities to persons authorized to perform state functions or persons equated to them, illegal material remuneration, gifts, benefits or services;

- carrying out illegal entrepreneurial activities outside the functions assigned to them by law and obtaining illegal income beyond the established sources of funding, state and local government bodies;

- failure of heads of state bodies to take measures within the limits of their authority against persons subordinate to them who are guilty of committing corruption offenses;

- hiring persons who have previously committed a corruption offense.

The penalties for these administrative corruption offenses vary:

- for individuals in the range from one hundred to six hundred monthly calculation indices;

- for legal entities - from seven hundred fifty (in case of a single violation) to one thousand five hundred monthly calculation indices (in case of a repeated violation within a year).

As can be seen from the above, the Republic of Kazakhstan has established a legal framework for anti-corruption efforts and the challenge is to ensure its strict and diligent application.

THEME 5. IMPROVEMENT OF SOCIO-ECONOMIC RELATIONS OF KAZAKHSTAN SOCIETY AS A CONDITION FOR COUNTERACTING CORRUPTION

Plan

1. Corruption risks in the socio-economic sector of modern Kazakhstan.
2. Main directions of improvement of socially economic relations in Kazakhstan.

1. Corruption risks in the socio-economic sector of modern Kazakhstan.

In modern Kazakhstan, corruption is a common phenomenon for both individual citizens and society as a whole, it remains the leading factor inhibiting the country's economic and social development; at the same time, there is a growing awareness among the population of corruption as a serious threat to national security and the perception is spreading that it is impossible to achieve success in combating this phenomenon through criminal punishments alone. In addition to legal measures, political, socio-economic and spiritual measures are necessary to successfully combat corruption. After all, modern corruption is a systemic, stable criminal phenomenon, which is based on economic, financial, informational, clan, ethnic, etc. ties and relations between representatives of state and local authorities and various criminal structures.

Socio-economic conditions of society have a determining influence on the level of corruption. At the same time, corruption, in turn, has an opposite effect on the socio-economic sphere.

In the social sphere, this impact is summarized as follows:

- corrupt relations create a gap between declared and real values, forming "double standards" of morality and behavior among members of society. In society there is a "planting of new moral values, the central place among which is occupied by the cult of personal prosperity and enrichment, and money is the measure and equivalent of life well-being"[51] . Corruption leads to the devaluation and breakdown of civilized social regulators of human behavior: norms of morality, law, religion, public opinion, etc. in society;
- corruption leads to a sharp increase in the social and property inequality of people, impoverishment of significant masses of the population, and the growth of social tension in the country;
- rampant corruption creates a perception among the population that ordinary citizens are defenseless against both the authorities and crime.

In the economic sphere, corruption causes the following negative consequences:

---

51 Kimlatsky O.A., Machulskaya I.G. On the state of the fight against corruption in the Russian Federation. http://www.
center-bereg.ru/m2648.html

- destroys the mechanism of market competition, giving advantages not to those who work efficiently and qualitatively, but to those who bribed, which ultimately leads to a decrease in the efficiency of the economy as a whole;

- leads to the embezzlement of public funds, in the distribution of state loans, preventing the implementation of state programs;

- causes inequitable distribution of income, enriching the corrupt at the expense of the rest of society;

- "overheads" spent on bribes are included in the cost of goods, causing prices to rise and ordinary consumers to suffer;

- corruption is a breeding ground for the spread of organized crime and the shadow economy.

There is no data on economic losses from corruption in Kazakhstan, but some insight can be gained from the following example: in Italy, following Operation Clean Hands against corruption, public expenditures on road construction decreased by 20%[52] .

It is well known that since independence our country has entered the stage of modernization of social, state and economic foundations. And today this process is far from over, which causes additional problems in combating corruption. Special literature on anti-corruption fight highlights the following problems common to countries at the stage of modernization that give rise to corruption[53] .

1) **Difficulties associated with overcoming the legacy of the totalitarian** system under which there was a centralized system of economic management. Interference of state authorities in the economy, especially at the regional level, is still significant, creating favorable conditions for corruption.

1. . **Economic decline and political instability** have caused a drop in the living standards of large segments of the population, as well as the inability of the state to provide civil servants with a decent living, which pushes both to mass grassroots corruption. This is facilitated by inflation, changing tax policy, constant government interference in the economy, and the lack of clear rules governing the relations of market actors. All this ultimately forms a certain stereotype of economic behavior oriented towards quick profit by any means, including corruption. Instability increases the scale of the shadow economy, expanding the scope of corruption.

3. **Underdeveloped and imperfect legislation, low legal culture not only of ordinary citizens, but also of government officials, including those of the highest rank.** This problem is associated primarily with the fact that modernization is accompanied by rapid changes in all spheres of society, while the legislative process always has a certain lag behind real life, creating a fertile ground for corruption. With the liberalization of the economy, the opportunities for officials of various ranks to influence economic processes have increased, using insufficiently elaborated legislation when granting various benefits, loans, licenses, privatization tenders,

52 Satarov G.A., Levin M.I. Russia and corruption: who is who? // Rossiyskaya Gazeta. 1998. February 19.
53 See: http://www.law.vl.ru/law/corrupt/index.html

implementation of social projects, etc. to economic entities.

4. **Inefficiency of the institutions of power**, manifested, first of all, in the fact that so far it has not yet been possible to create a coherent state system that would ensure strict compliance with the proclaimed rules of the market economy. The lack of effective protection from the state forces economic entities to seek it from specific officials, establishing corrupt ties.

The nomenklatura system of guilds in the selection and promotion of civil servants, left over from the totalitarian system, has not yet been completely destroyed. There are still a lot of swindlers who enter the civil service with a specific goal: to use it for personal enrichment.

5. **Weakness of civil society, separation of society from the authorities**. In the previous lectures it was shown that successful fight against corruption is possible only if the state closely cooperates with civil society institutions. However, the inevitable decline in the socio-political status of citizens accompanying the initial period of transition to the process of modernization of society causes disappointment replacing former hopes, which contributes to the alienation of society from the authorities and a decrease in the activity of public associations.

The weakness of civil society in Kazakhstan is also related to the fact that, as in the entire territory of the former Soviet Union, civil society institutions were virtually non-existent at the time of the declaration of independence, and today the process of their creation and inclusion in the political life of the country is far from over.

These and other reasons create conditions for corruption risks[54] , the main ones being.

1. **Privatizations of state property.** Large-scale privatization took place in the 1990s and early 2000s, but even today there are still significant objects subject to privatization in Kazakhstan, the third wave of which is announced for early 2016. The most common types of corruption in this area are embezzlement and bribery. In the course of privatization, a large number of corrupt practices that do not fall under direct criminal liability are committed, such as undervaluation of privatized objects, manipulation of tender conditions, and buying up enterprises by officials through proxies.

2. **Distribution of budget funds.** The chronic shortage of budget funds gives officials the opportunity to decide who to allocate funds to in full and who to give not in full, who to transfer money to earlier and who to later, which is accompanied by corruption.

Budgetary funds are also distributed through state orders and procurement. This sphere is still the most closed and uncontrolled in the distribution and use of public funds, even in the Armed Forces, as evidenced by the 2014-2015 trials of former high-ranking officials of the Ministry of Defense of the Republic of Kazakhstan.

3. **Granting privileges** on exports and imports, taxes, licensing, etc. This also

54 Corruption risk is the possibility of occurrence of causes and conditions conducive to the commission of corruption offenses.

includes deferrals of tax payments, extension of loan agreements, provision of state guarantees, budgetary preferences used to obtain bribes.

4. **Banking sector.** The transfer of budget funds to the management of commercial banks is a source of enormous profits for them in conditions of high inflation and opens wide opportunities for corruption.

5. **Law enforcement agencies,** merging with economic crime, create an environment that generates a variety of corrupt practices: direct extortion by law enforcement officials, their pressure for bribes on competitors in the commercial sphere, making money from the collapse of criminal cases, patronage ("roofing") of illegal businesses, and much more.

6. **The sphere of taxation** creates a favorable breeding ground for corruption. The following are widespread here: rewriting of inspection acts, issuing fictitious certificates for the benefit of commercial structures, direct counseling on tax evasion.

7. **Customs** is one of the most attractive sectors for corruption. It is associated with the movement of a large number of goods, the clearance of which requires considerable time and money to pay customs duties. Corruption schemes make it possible to do it faster and cheaper, causing multi-billion dollar losses for the state budget. The scale of corruption in the customs service of the Republic of Kazakhstan is illustrated by past court proceedings in the so-called "Khorgos case".

8. **Conscription for military service.** Bribery for the opportunity to be exempted from conscription is widespread here. According to some data[55] in Russia, more than half of the young men who were exempted from military conscription achieved it with the help of bribes.

High probability of corruption risks is also associated with such actions as:

- collection of fines and other payments from the public by various agencies;
- issuance of permits to engage in various types of activities;
- building permits and land vesting;
- control by state services (fire, sanitary, etc.), from which small and medium-sized businesses in Kazakhstan suffer.

When authorities interact with ordinary citizens, the emergence of corruption risks is facilitated by[56] :

- maintaining a wide range of public services covered by the permit principle;
- Citizens' ignorance of their rights to receive services and officials' obligations to provide them;
- concealment by officials of information about their duties and rights of citizens;
- the complexity of bureaucratic procedures;

55 See: http://www.law.vl.ru/law/corrupt/index.html

56 See: ibid.

- The monopoly of agencies to provide services;
- structural features of the authorities, where one agency has the authority to both make power decisions and provide services.

In this interaction, corruption risks are also associated with the lack of convenient procedures for citizens to realize their obligations (for example, the prospect of going to the bank and standing in line to pay a fine for a traffic violation is likely to force a citizen to bribe an inspector - it will be cheaper and reduce time).

2. Main directions of improvement of socio-economic relations in Kazakhstan

Starting from the moment of achieving independence and up to the present time, Kazakhstan has passed a number of stages on the way to creating a democratic, secular, legal and social state with a developed market economy, a state whose highest values are a human being, his life, rights and freedoms, as proclaimed in the Constitution. At each of these stages, specific tasks were solved, the realization of which moved the country in the specified direction; and the stages themselves, their concretization, tasks and goals were formulated in the annual Addresses of the President N.A.Nazarbayev to the people of Kazakhstan: it is the President's constitutional duty to determine the main directions of domestic and foreign policy of the state[57] .

In 1997, President Nazarbayev in his Address "Prosperity, security and improvement of welfare of all Kazakhstanis" presented the Development Strategy of the Republic of Kazakhstan until 2030 (Strategy "Kazakhstan-2030"), which outlined the long-term path of the country's development aimed at transforming the Republic of Kazakhstan into one of the safest, stable, economically stable states in the world with a dynamically developing economy.

The Kazakhstan-2030 Development Strategy provides for the realization of seven long-term priorities, two of which (3 and 7) are directly related to the topic of our lecture:

3. Economic growth based on an open market economy with high levels of foreign investment and domestic savings. -

7. Professional State.

The realization of the third priority is based on ten basic principles, the most important of which are: "Limited government intervention in the economy with an active role. The strategy to address these problems is to: eliminate the government's still existing administrative interference in trade and production; complete the privatization process, including real estate, the remaining small and medium-sized enterprises and agro-industry; organize and simplify the central government and local governments wisely, seriously rethinking their roles, powers and responsibilities; vigorously pursue the reform of the judiciary and law enforcement agencies; establish the absolute rule of law and protect law-abiding citizens

---

[57] See: Constitution of the Republic of Kazakhstan. Art. 40.1.

On the contrary, to apply the full force of power and the law to those who provide themselves a trouble-free existence by illegal means"[58] . It is clear that the elimination of administrative interference in business significantly narrows the field of action of corrupt officials.

The realization of the seventh priority to create a professional state explicitly sets the task of decisively and ruthlessly fighting corruption and improving the system of recruitment, training and promotion.

Speaking in October 2007 at the international conference dedicated to the 10th anniversary of the Strategy "Kazakhstan-2030", Mr. Nazarbayev noted that one of the main long-term priorities for Kazakhstan remains the improvement of the efficiency of public administration. Over the past decade during the implementation of the Strategy "the Agency for Civil Service was created, the Laws "On Civil Service", "On Combating Corruption", "On Administrative Procedures", the Code of Honor of Civil Servants were adopted. A competitive system of recruitment to the civil service was introduced. Some functions not peculiar to the state have been transferred to the competitive environment. In accordance with the latest constitutional amendments, local power has been strengthened and maslikhats have been empowered with the powers of local self-government bodies.

... According to the assessment of international organizations and experts, Kazakhstan has achieved high results in the field of civil service reform, bringing its legislation and procedures closer to international standards.

But we still have a lot to do in this area. And the Government on my instruction is actively working to continue administrative reform"[59] .

In the same year, in his regular Address, the President identified 30 major areas of our domestic and foreign policy, among which an important place is given to combating corruption. In particular, the task is to develop and implement measures to support small and medium-sized businesses, to identify and reduce legislative, administrative and bureaucratic obstacles to business initiative. The government has been tasked to "conduct a comprehensive revision of antimonopoly legislation and create clear mechanisms for identifying the facts of restriction of competition and collusion between market participants, preventing "hidden" monopolization of the basic sectors of our economy, as well as appropriate recommendations on the application of penalties"[60] . The tasks of simplification of procedures **for** registration of land plots, as well as transparency of the procedure of their provision, transfer of all non-strategic types of economic activities of the state into a competitive-market environment have been set. The creation of the so-called "electronic government" will have an impact on the reduction of contacts of civil servants with the population, which create corruption risks.

---

58 Kazakhstan 2030. Development Strategy of Kazakhstan until 2030: problems and ways of their realization. http://www.tarih-begalinka.kz/ru/history/independent/history/page3385/

59 Kazakhstan-2030 Strategy in action: 10 years of success. http://dppzhambyl.gov.kz/strategy 2030.php

60 Message of the President of the Republic of Kazakhstan N. Nazarbayev to the people of Kazakhstan. February 28, 2007. http://shahtinsk.gov.kz/ru/pos_6_5

Step-by-step progress of Kazakhstan in the direction of implementation of the Strategy "Kazakhstan-2030", solution of some or other tasks cause the necessity of revision and concretization of the current legislation. In particular, by 2008 there was a need to bring the existing tax system in line with the current economic realities. As noted in the Presidential Address of February 6, 2008, "the current Tax Code has played a positive role in economic growth, but at present its potential is practically exhausted. The Code has over 170 types of benefits and preferences, which are constantly and haphazardly growing. The government should develop a new Tax Code. It should contribute to the modernization and diversification of the economy, the exit of business from the "shadow".

The new Code should acquire the character of a law of direct action, protecting from free interpretation of its norms by tax services, combining the quality of administration and the interests of taxpayers"[61] .

The new realities required improvement of legislation, primarily with regard to competition and the fight against crime and corruption. The Agency for the Protection of Competition was established to fight price collusion, unfair competition, and abuse by market players of their dominant and monopolistic position.

The Address devotes considerable attention to the problem of accelerated implementation of measures envisaged by the administrative reform to develop the system of public administration on the principles of efficiency, transparency and accountability to society, taking into account the best international experience. One of the key elements of the administrative reform, the President emphasizes, "should be a new personnel policy in the country. The human factor becomes decisive at the modern stage of development. It is necessary to develop modern approaches aimed at the formation of a professional core of managers of a new formation in the system of public administration"[62] .

Another problem in this area is reducing the administrative burden on business, further simplifying the permitting system and, above all, licensing, certification and accreditation. The President shows how serious this problem is by citing the following

the following example: "According to the World Bank's latest Doing Business report, it takes 89 days to complete all export procedures in Kazakhstan, while in Estonia, for example, it takes only 5 days. A real disaster for an entrepreneur is various kinds of inspections, which are stipulated by over 50 laws! Some agencies seek an opportunity to "check" the company several times under various pretexts in violation of the law. This seriously distracts businesses from their business. And this goes against the policy I am pursuing. It is necessary to significantly reduce the number of inspections by law enforcement and other inspection agencies, and to streamline them"[63] .

For ten years of implementation of the Strategy "Kazakhstan-2030" "we have doubled

---

61 Message of the President of the Republic of Kazakhstan N. Nazarbayev to the people of Kazakhstan. February 6, 2008. http://shahtinsk.gov.kz/ru/pos_6_4
62 Ibid.
63 Message of the President of the Republic of Kazakhstan N. Nazarbayev to the people of Kazakhstan. February 6, 2008. http://shahtinsk.gov.kz/ru/pos_6_4

the volume of GDP of the republic, and effectively fulfilled the social obligations of the state. The average monthly salary has increased 5 times, and the average size of pensions 3 times. The share of the population with incomes below the subsistence minimum has decreased 4 times (from 50% to 12%). The main health indicators of the population have improved. Life expectancy increased from 65 to 68 years. Maternal mortality has halved and the birth rate has increased one and a half times"[64] .

The next step in the socio-economic development of Kazakhstan was the adoption and implementation of the Strategic Plan - 2020, outlined in the Presidential Address of January 29, 2010 "A New Decade - New Economic Growth - New Opportunities for Kazakhstan". In this Address, a threefold task was put forward: "first, to significantly improve the business climate; second, to ensure the stable functioning of the financial system; third, to continue the formation of a reliable legal environment"[65] .

The solution of this task, noted in the Address, will allow Kazakhstan to enter the list of 50 countries with the most favorable business climate.

Implementation of the Strategic Plan 2020 sets new tasks of strengthening the economy and improving the welfare of the people. These tasks were formulated in the President's Address of January 27, 2012 and their solution should, according to the President's plan, determine the main vector of socio-economic development of Kazakhstan for the next decade.

The first of these tasks is the employment of Kazakhstanis. The country has developed and started to implement the Employment Program aimed at creating an effective system of training and employment assistance, promoting entrepreneurship in rural areas, increasing the mobility of labor resources, and priority employment in the centers of economic activity of Kazakhstan.

Another task is to improve the quality of public services to the population. The solution of this task is an important aspect of combating corruption and increasing the confidence of citizens in the activities of state bodies. The central link in solving this task is further improvement of the work of the "electronic government". The Address sets a specific task: by the end of 2012, 60 percent of socially important public services, including all types of licenses, should be provided only in electronic form.

In his Address, the President once again returns to the tasks of improving the system of training a qualified political class of managers and staff selection, modernizing the judicial and law enforcement systems. Speaking about the fight against corruption, the President for the first time raises the issue of the transition to declaring not only the income but also the expenses of civil servants, as well as the need to develop a Comprehensive Anti-Corruption Program.

The assessment of the results of socio-economic development of Kazakhstan over the past 20 years of independence was given by President Nazarbayev in the Address of December 14, 2012 "Strategy "Kazakhstan-2050". New political course of the

---

64 Message of the President of the Republic of Kazakhstan N. Nazarbayev to the people of Kazakhstan. January 29, 2010. http://shahtinsk.gov.kz/ru/pos_6_2
65 Ibid.

established state". In this Address, the main goal of Kazakhstan's development for the next period is defined - to become **one of the 30 most developed countries in the world** by 2050, creating a **welfare society based on a strong state, developed economy and opportunities for universal labor.**

The main results of the twenty-year development of Kazakhstan, noted in the Address, are[66] :

- Creation of a strong independent state based on a modern system of governance;
- A sustainable process of democratization and liberalization linked to the level of economic development;
- harmony and peace among different social, ethnic and religious groups;
- modern model of market economy based on private property, free competition and principles of openness;
- strong social policies that have ensured social stability and harmony;
- Kazakhstan is recognized by the international community as a responsible and reliable partner.

During the implementation of the Strategy "Kazakhstan-2030" the country's GDP has increased more than 16 times, the volume of industrial production - 20 times, more than 44 thousand new jobs have been created. The average monthly salary increased 9.3 times. The average size of pension payments increased 10 times, life expectancy rose to 70 years. Nominal monetary incomes of the population increased 16 times.

The analysis of the results of Kazakhstan's development over the past time gave the President grounds to conclude that "the main tasks set by the Strategy-2030 have been accomplished, others are in the process of implementation" and to justify the need to "build a **new political course of the nation until 2050,** within which the implementation of the tasks of **the** Strategy-2030 will continue"[67] .

The main goals of further development of Kazakhstan are defined in the Address:

- further development and strengthening of statehood;
- transition to new principles of economic policy;
- comprehensive support for entrepreneurship - the leading force of the national economy;
- the formation of a new social model;
- Creation of modern and effective education and health care systems;
- increasing the responsibility, efficiency and functionality of the state apparatus;
- building an international and defense policy adequate to the new challenges.

---

66 See: Address of the President of the Republic of Kazakhstan N. Nazarbayev to the people of Kazakhstan, December 14, 2012 http://shahtinsk.gov.kz/ru/pos_6_17.

67 Address of the President of the Republic of Kazakhstan N. Nazarbayev to the people of Kazakhstan, December 14, 2012. http://shahtinsk.gov.kz/ru/pos_6_17

The Strategy "Kazakhstan-2050", which defines the main directions of the country's progressive movement towards these goals, is dedicated to the achievement of these goals.

First of all, the Strategy elaborates in detail the New Deal economic policy - **comprehensive economic pragmatism based on the principles of profitability, return on investment and competitiveness.** The main thing in this policy is to create a favorable investment climate in order to build up economic potential and an efficient private sector of the economy. It is easy to see that both the former and the latter are possible only with an active reduction of the corruption component.

In the Address, the President again draws attention to the need to continue liberalizing tax and systematizing customs administration.

An important place in the Strategy is given to comprehensive support of entrepreneurship, which the President called "the driving force of the new economic course". At the same time, speaking of the need to "create conditions for a person to try his or her hand at business, to become a **full-fledged participant in the economic transformations underway in the country**, and not to expect the state to solve all the problems for him or her," the President points out that for this purpose, among other things, it is necessary to "envisage the introduction of a new, **stricter system of responsibility** for state officials who create artificial obstacles for business. Here the President also instructs the Government "to **cancel all permits and licenses** that do not directly affect the **safety of life of citizens of Kazakhstan and** replace them with notifications by the end of the first half of 2013".

Based on the well-known, confirmed by international experience, provision on the greater efficiency of private business compared to state business, the Address sets the task of conducting the second wave of large-scale privatization (in parentheses, we note that the third wave of privatization began on January 1, 2016). "This," the Address notes, "is not an easy step, as it will mean a redistribution of **responsibility between the state and the market.** But we must take it in order to maintain high rates of economic growth".

The Address formulates the basic principles of the new social policy, the essence of which is summarized as follows:

- guaranteeing citizens a minimum social standard;
- Providing social support only to those groups that need it;
- elimination of social imbalances in the development of regions;
- modernization of employment and remuneration policies.

Speaking about the task of forming a professional state apparatus for which "**service to the people and the state is paramount," the** President paid special attention to the new civil service system, which would ensure "strengthening anti-corruption measures, increasing transparency in the selection of civil servants, and introducing the principle of meritocracy, i.e. promoting the best personnel.

The implementation of these and other provisions of the Kazakhstan-2050 Strategy has been complicated by the global crisis, which has led to a slowdown in economic growth worldwide and a collapse in world markets. This, emphasized in the Presidential Address of November 30, 2015 "Kazakhstan in the New Global Reality: Growth, Reforms, Development", has caused the need to develop an anti-crisis strategy based on three concepts[68] :

- growth, first of all, of the economy through the disclosure of private initiative;
- reforms based on the developed document "Plan of the Nation. One hundred concrete steps".
- development, continuous modernization of all spheres of society.

The anti-crisis strategy envisages structural changes in the following five areas:

- stabilization of the financial sector;
- optimization of budgetary policy;
- privatization and promotion of economic competition;
- new investment policy;
- new social policy.

As we can see, the five directions of anti-crisis transformations defined in the Address represent further development and concretization, as well as adjustment, in relation to new conditions, of the plans of Kazakhstan's transit movement towards a democratic, secular, legal and social state.

68 See: Address of the President of the Republic of Kazakhstan N. Nazarbayev to the people of Kazakhstan. 30.11.2015 http://www.adilet.gov.kz/ru/node/109370

TOPIC 6. PSYCHOLOGICAL PECULIARITIES OF THE NATURE OF CORRUPT BEHAVIOR

Plan

1. Psychological factors of corruption.
2. Personal determinants of corrupt behavior.

1. Psychological factors of corruption

Corruption is a multidimensional, multilevel, systematically organized social phenomenon, which, in addition to economic, legal, social, managerial, ethical and political, has a psychological component. Bribes are taken and given, abused, etc. by living people with their passions and urges, so measures to combat this phenomenon should take into account the need to address the most important issues of individual psychological and socio-psychological nature.

Social psychological studies of corrupt behavior identify two leading motives[69] :

- the pursuit of material goods;
- attitude towards corruption as a dangerous and exciting game.

The first of them - visible, external - is self-interest, the desire to provide oneself with material benefits, to satisfy one's exorbitant material needs and ambitions. Often illegal obtaining of material benefits becomes an end in itself without a clear idea of what such means are needed for.

The second - deep - semantic motive of corruption lies in the realization of game motives. Many corrupt individuals are players by nature, and they do not realize this attraction in any way and it functions in the unconscious sphere of their psyche. They enter the game in complex, emotionally colored situations; they cannot imagine themselves outside of such a game, playing with other people, with danger, with the law, with their own fate. This brings them great psychological satisfaction

As Y.M. Antonyan emphasizes, "game motives in corrupt behavior are intertwined with selfish motives and begin to powerfully determine each other. The presence of these two bases of motivation and their mutual strengthening largely explains both the prevalence of corruption and the fact that the corresponding behaviour is implemented over many years, becoming a way of life"[70] . Researchers note that the most successful in corruption frauds are people with creative thinking, who like to take risks and are characterized by unconventional thinking[71] .

The most common motives for corruption determined by psychological factors are[72] :

69 See: Antonyan Y.M. Typology of corruption and corrupt behavior [Electronic resource]. - URL: http://antonyan-jm.narod.ru/inter3.html.

70 Ibid.

71 See: Psychologists have studied the causes of corruption [Electronic resource]. - URL: http://elizaveta-mc.ru/blogs/tag/%D0%BF%D1%81%D0%B8%D1%85 %D0%BE%D0%BB%D0%B

72 See: Sazonova N.P. Psychological aspects of corruption [Electronic resource] - https://www. google.kz/?client=opera&gws_rd=cr&ei=rEryVuXpH-P5yQOpl56YCQ

- Compensation for the perceived damage to the official's service.
- a sense of instability;
- Low wages that do not match the qualifications and responsibility of the job;
- unfairness in promotions;
- rudeness or incompetence of a superior.

In the socio-psychological analysis of corruption, the attitude towards this phenomenon, which is directly related to the mass psychology of citizens, is of great importance. This attitude in modern Kazakhstan manifests itself in three ways: first, as tolerance, i.e. an attitude to corruption as an inevitable and invincible evil that does not deserve condemnation ("who does not take it?", "to be in the water and not get wet?"); second, condemnation in the mass consciousness not of corruption in general, but of the most large-scale cases; third, an inconsistent and contradictory attitude based on a system of double moral standards. On the one hand, corruption, especially top corruption, is considered socially unacceptable. On the other hand, corruption, especially grassroots corruption, is practically not condemned and even justified. "I and my relatives committed a corrupt act as a response to objective circumstances, while similar actions of other persons are condemned".

The spread of corruption is also significantly influenced by such social and psychological peculiarities of our society as the priority of informal ties and relations over formal ones. The unexpired vestiges of patriarchal elements, such as cronyism, nepotism, etc., are characteristic of our society and pose a massive corruption threat. - are characteristic of our society and create a massive corruption threat. It is not by chance that wives of high officials often become "successful entrepreneurs" earning many times more than their high-ranking spouses. There are many examples when relatives of high officials, regardless of their qualifications, suddenly turn out to be heads of solid institutions and organizations. In other words, the habit of achieving something by blat, acquaintance or kinship is firmly rooted in the mentality of our society. It is this circumstance that has formed a well-known model of behavior, when a person who committed, for example, a traffic accident, begins to call first of all not the traffic police, and not the ambulance to help the injured, but the right people who could "get him off".

Informal relations prevailing in our society have led to the formation of various corruption networks, when, for example, police officers of one district, "roofing" retail outlets, share the proceeds of corruption with their partners who did not take part in a particular action. Or when lower ranks share corruption money with their superiors, which is more dangerous for society.

The creation of corrupt networks creates a social and psychological environment in which even the most honest person can remain in it only by becoming corrupt. Otherwise, the network "gets rid" of him, rejects him. "In certain segments of society that have turned into corruption testing grounds, formal recruitment procedures are already an admission to corrupt systems. Closed procedures of personnel selection contribute to the fact that subjects knowingly ready for corrupt practices are admitted to service in corrupt systems"[73] .

Participation in corruption networks also has such a negative socio-psychological effect as the loss of a sense of responsibility for committed acts, which ultimately leads to the expansion and deepening of corruption. "The subjective perception of risk is reduced if an official shares a bribe with his superiors, a salesman gives part of the kickback to the head of the firm. And the more numerous the network of participants in a corrupt transaction, the less the sense of guilt ... and the risk of ruining one's reputation if exposed"[74] .

And one more negative point in the socio-psychological state of our society should be mentioned - the lack of a clear understanding of the boundary between a bribe and gratitude. The majority of our citizens believe that some types of services imply gratitude in a commodity-money form, clearly realizing that the addressee does not demand anything from him in return. For example, to a teacher or university professor for a good grade in an exam, to a doctor for a successful operation, etc. Most citizens perceive these actions as natural human gratitude, not as a corrupt act. Meanwhile, in the culture of many nations such forms of behavior cause incomprehension and bewilderment: they are considered wild and offensive. In other words, many actions characterized (and punished) as corrupt in other countries are considered normal and commonplacc in our socicty. Corruption, in its broadest interpretation, is our way of life today. According to numerous surveys, there is practically none among citizens who would not give bribes in one form or another. At the same time, the number of corrupt offers far exceeds the number of bribe extortions, i.e. citizens often impose bribes on officials themselves, even though they do not demand it.

Socio-psychological factors of corruption are significantly influenced by the transitional nature of modern Kazakhstani society, where the formation of new forms of social relations lags behind the political and economic activity of the population, when the institutionalization of new forms has not yet been enshrined in laws and the adoption of relevant decisions is completely dependent on the arbitrariness of officials. Hence, an important direction in the fight against corruption is to radically reduce the number of permissive and prohibitive functions of officials. A significant influence on the spread of corruption is the indifference of a significant part of Kazakhstani society to violations of social norms and mass cynicism towards antisocial offenses. The level of corruption is influenced by various features of national culture (e.g., the tradition of gift-giving), its peculiarities such as collectivism or individualism, peculiarities of religious confessions, etc.

From the above, we can conclude that corruption is a culturally conditioned phenomenon, "constantly reproduced by cultural tradition, relying on permanent, stable features of national culture"[75] .

---

73 Alekseev S.V. Corruption in the transition society [Electronic resource] . - URL: http://www. ceninauku.ru/page_23202.htm.

74 Glinkina S.P. Corruption: a fatal threat? // Non-economic facets of the economy: unrecognized mutual influence / ed. by O.T. Bogomolov. - M., 2010. C. 443.

75 Nestik T.A. Corruption and culture [Electronic resource] // Shadow economy in Soviet and post-Soviet

The previous topics have already discussed ways to counteract corruption, among which legislative measures have an important place and should be complemented by other measures, in particular those related to psychology.

Among such measures, the first place is occupied by the will of the authorities, the state and society as a whole to uncompromisingly fight corruption. And here it should be noted that today in most post-Soviet countries there is a lack of will for this fight. As Y.Y. Boldyrev notes, "the problem is not that no one knows what to do, but that neither the authorities nor society have the main thing - the will to solve the problem"[76] . The situation is further complicated by the fact that corruption is primarily to be fought by officials, most of whom are themselves corrupt, while civil society in our country is not yet strong enough to force officials to fight this phenomenon.

At the same time, it is obvious that the fight against corruption cannot be reduced to the efforts of the authorities and officials alone; it must be of a mass nature, involving broad segments of the population and based on appropriate behavioral practices. This requires a change in the tolerant attitude of the majority of Kazakhstani society towards corruption as a minor evil, inevitable and inexorable. It is necessary to develop mass awareness of the harmfulness of corrupt behavior, even in the most seemingly innocuous cases. Recent history is full of examples when everyday corruption, perceived as minor deviations, led to terrible tragedies (remember the unimpeded passage of militants through traffic police checkpoints for the terrorist attack on the school in the city of Beslan, the penetration of terrorist women, bypassing checkpoints, to the airplane they blew up over Voronezh, etc.).

From a psychological point of view, there are two forms of participation in anti-corruption activities for ordinary citizens who are not burdened with any authority - passive and active.

The essence of **the passive form** lies in the well-known expression "simply not giving bribes". This peculiar form of anti-corruption fight requires a certain determination from the subject, as well as willingness to give up certain material or non-material (e.g. acceleration of obtaining a permit thanks to a bribe) benefits. This form of fight is usually publicly approved and supported by the public.

Another form of ordinary citizens' fight against corruption is **active** - it consists of complaints (signals, statements) to the competent authorities about bribe-takers or those who live beyond their means. As a rule, this type of struggle in our society is condemned and is mostly qualified as "denunciation", "sexploitation", or "gossip". This mass negative attitude towards "informers" has its historical roots, but it is also connected with modern reasons: citizens' disbelief in the interest of the authorities in eradicating corruption, distrust in law enforcement agencies, unwillingness to take responsibility in long-lasting proceedings on a complaint. The "blatnaya" romance and "notions" of the criminal world, which have taken deep roots especially among today's

---

societies. 2002. № 4. - URL: http://corruption.rsuh.ru/magazine/3/n4- 05.html.

76 Boldyrev Y.Y. Corruption as a systemic vice of Russian capitalism // Non-economic facets of the economy: unrecognized mutual influence / edited by O.T. Bogomolov. - Moscow: Institute of Economic Strategies, 2010, p. 456.

young generation, have also played their role in the negative attitude of society towards complaints. The passivity of citizens is also greatly influenced by the fact that, according to the existing legislation, anonymous complaints to various authorities are not subject to consideration.

This negative approach to "denunciation" in our country contrasts vividly with what happens in such a case in Western countries. If there, says one source, "one parks a car in an inappropriate place, several people will report it to the police, who will come immediately, and what we call denunciation is perceived as the fulfillment of civic duty, receives the full support of others and is encouraged in every possible way, including financially"[77] .

In low-corruption countries, the technology of filing and responding to citizens' complaints is simplified to the extreme. Here, in any institution where there are corruption risks, the most prominent places are marked with addresses, including e-mail addresses, and telephone numbers of services where complaints should be filed, including anonymously. There is no need to write personal statements, which our fellow citizens are very afraid of, nor to lose time waiting in line to see those responsible for fighting corruption, nor to spend envelopes on postage. It is important that the criminal punishment of corrupt officials is accompanied by their inclusion in "black lists", which then prevents them from taking any public office for the rest of their lives. And this is against the backdrop of the Kazakhstani reality, where officials found guilty of corruption are again employed in high, including public, positions and do not suffer from remorse.

In recent years, the issue of introducing polygraphs ("lie detectors") into the practice of personnel selection in government structures has been gaining resonance in society. Although experts recognize the positive effect of the introduction of this device and it is already being used in some structures, it would be premature to talk about its widespread use in the anti-corruption fight.

2. Personal determinants of corrupt behavior

The problem of corruption in modern society has acquired an important practical significance, which has made it necessary to take cardinal measures to counteract this phenomenon. This, in turn, has given rise to numerous studies on economic, legal, and social aspects of corruption, which, according to the generally recognized opinion, should also take into account the psychological aspect. As M. Reshetnikov notes, "without psychologically grounded approaches, it is unlikely that anything can be done here, because corruption is only a legal and economic problem in its consequences, but initially it is a purely psychological and human problem"[78] .

To analyze and characterize the psychological aspects of corruption, psychological science uses the following concepts: "corrupt behavior", "corruption pressure", "anti-

---

77 A. L. Zhuravlev, A. V. Yurevich. Psychological factors of corruption [Electronic resource] - http://www.ulan-ude-eg.ru/information/anticorruption/komissiya/Psih%20 faktori.pdf

78 Reshetnikov M. Psychology of corruption: utopia and dystopia. SPb.: East European Institute of Psychoanalysis, 2008, p. 107.

corruption resistance", "propensity to corruption"[79] .

Corrupt behavior is the behavior of an official aimed at obtaining a personal benefit through abuse of office.

Corruption pressure is a set of social and psychological factors of influence on an official, leading to a situation of choice between abuse of power for personal gain or rejection of it.

Anti-corruption resilience is a systemic property of an individual manifested in the ability to resist corruption pressure and to choose between criminal and law-abiding behavior in favor of the latter.

Corruption propensity is a personal predisposition to choose corrupt behavior in a situation of corrupt pressure.

From the psychological point of view, it is extremely important to identify the personal determinants of corrupt behavior of officials, to answer the question: what determines the behavior of a corrupt official - external factors (corruption pressure) or internal properties of the personality (propensity to corruption or anti-corruption resistance).

In its essence, corrupt behavior is a type of social behavior, as it is an action of an official that affects the interests of individuals, social groups, communities or society as a whole. It manifests individual psychological and social qualities of a person, such as temperament, character, will, motivations, professional and moral beliefs, and value orientations.

On the other hand, corrupt behavior is a type of deviant behavior determined by the compliance or non-compliance of certain actions with professional norms and social expectations. However, it should be borne in mind that in structures where corruption has become widespread and systemic, corrupt behavior may be regarded as a "norm", while conscientious and honest performance by officials of their official duties may be regarded as deviant behavior.

When analyzing the psychological aspects of corrupt activities, it is important to identify personal properties that increase the likelihood of corrupt behavior in a situation of choice. Together, these properties are defined by the concept of **a "corruption-prone personality",** which means a certain type of personality with a high propensity to corruption and low anti-corruption resistance. Such a personality is more likely to choose corrupt behavior in the conditions of corruption pressure, while refusal from it in these conditions will have a very low probability for him/her. As noted in the literature, "no external circumstances can be the determining causes of an unlawful act unless they are simultaneously placed on the internal determinants of human activity"[80] . In other words, when characterizing corrupt acts, it is always necessary, along with the action of external causes (corruption risks), to always keep

---

79 See: Vannovskaya O.V. Personal determinants of corrupt behavior [Electronic resource]. http://cyberleninka.ru/article/n/lichnostnye-determinanty-korruptsionnogo- povedeniya#ixzz3vax3DIta

80 Lyskov B. D., Kurbatova T. N. Notion of the personality of a criminal // Legal Psychology / comp. and ed. by T. N. Kurbatova. SPb.: Peter, 2001, p. 77.

in mind a set of significant specific properties of the personality of the subject of these acts, i.e. certain internal determinants of a corrupt personality.

What properties underlie a corruption-prone personality? Researchers note that these properties are determined by factors located at different behavioral levels of personality. O.V. Vannovskaya identifies five levels of personality formations underlying the formation of a corruption-prone personality[81] .

1. **The level of meanings and values.** What is the meaning of a corrupt person's actions? Why does he need proof of his importance in the form of corruption proceeds? What makes him strive to achieve significant material benefits? What is the meaning of life for him? Answers to these questions help to understand the semantic component of a corrupt individual's behavior. It is clear that for this type of personality the meaning-forming component of behavior is the acquisition of wealth. Thus, the value orientations and life ideals that form the meaningful side of the personality's orientation and express the inner basis of its attitude to reality are reduced for a corrupt person to the predominance of material, rather than spiritual values. For such a person, the measure of happiness and good is wealth, luxury, money, and the leading value is the value "To Have" rather than the value "To Be" (E. Fromm).

2. **Cognitive-moral level.** This level includes attitudes of moral behavior, i.e. individual, moral, social and legal attitudes. If individual attitudes prevail in the determinants of moral behavior, anti-corruption resistance will be the highest, as these attitudes are immanent to the personality, are individual norms of behavior, i.e. they represent the most stable characteristics in human behavior. If moral or social determinants prevail in a person's behavior, anti-corruption resistance will be lower, because here he/she will be guided by the morals and attitudes of the surrounding society. The indicators of anti-corruption resistance will be lower when legal determinants prevail, because the main regulator of moral behavior here are the principles of encouragement and punishment external to the individual, established by laws, which are perceived as external and alien for the majority of our citizens. As A.I.Kirpichnikov notes, "historically there has been ... a view of the law as a kind of external, morally unsupported force that arbitrarily creates prohibitions and compels compliance with them"[82] . If none of the four attitudes can dominate, a person's propensity to corruption increases.

3. **The emotional level** implies several indicators that are relevant for determining the propensity to corruption - these are "life satisfaction, satisfaction with profession, satisfaction with personal status and self-relationship"[83] . The research has revealed a correlation between the level of life satisfaction and anti-corruption resistance of a personality. The higher the level of life satisfaction, the higher the anti-corruption resistance and vice versa. The same correlation can be traced between the level of satisfaction with profession, satisfaction with personal status and the level of anti-

81 See: Vannovskaya O.V. op. cit. op. cit.
82 Kirpichnikov A. I. Russian Corruption. 3rd edition, revised and supplemented. St. Petersburg: Legal Center Press, 2004, p. 214.
83 Vannovskaya O.V. op. cit. op. cit.

corruption resistance.

4. The **regulatory level** is connected with the **locus of control** indicator, which is understood as a person's tendency to see the source of control over his/her life either mainly in the external environment or in himself/herself[84] . There are two types of locus of control - internal and external. In the first case (internal locus), the individual takes responsibility for the events of his life on himself. In the second case (external locus), the individual attributes all responsibility to external factors (other people, chance, environment, etc.). It is obvious that a corrupt person has an external locus of control, while a person with high anti-corruption resistance has an internal locus of control.

5. **The behavioral level** is associated with two main types of response: impulsive and reflexive. In the impulsive type, the reaction to external stimuli is spontaneous and emotional. In the case of the reflexive type of reaction, a person's actions are mediated by a logical analysis of the situation. It is obvious that a person with the leading impulsive type of reaction will be more inclined to corrupt actions, and a person with the leading reflexive type will be less inclined.

Based on the above characteristics, a psychological portrait of a corruption-prone personality has been formed. "It is characterized by: comprehension of life through the acquisition of material goods, desire for luxury as an indicator of happiness, unconscious motivation and undifferentiated structure of attitudes of moral behavior, low level of life satisfaction, negative self-relationship and inadequate self-esteem, external locus of control, impulsive type of reaction"[85] .

The classification of types of bribe takers based on personal determinants of corrupt behavior is of certain interest[86]

Active bribe taker - is characterized by legal nihilism, stable anti-social attitudes. Has an inner drive to bribery. Actively creates artificial situations conducive to bribery. The main motive for corrupt actions is self-interest. At the same time, he/she may be pushed to commit a crime by the desire to show his/her superiority over other people, his/her power and importance. Usually, such people have a desire for a relevant position based on the intention to engage in bribery.

Habitual bribe taker - has contradictory, unstable moral and psychological attitudes, low level of legal awareness and legal culture. This type, unlike the active type, does not artificially create situations that provoke bribery; he does it because of habit, the existing "rules" in the organization. As in the first case, the main motive for committing a crime is self-interest.

Situational bribe-taker (unstable type) - here also the motive of the crime is self-interest. A bribe-taker of this type does not have strong anti-social attitudes, at the same time, his personal socio-psychological properties are unstable, his attitude to social

84 See: Bazhin E. F., Golynkina E. A. A., Etkind A. M. Questionnaire of the level of subjective control (USK). Moscow: Smysl, 1993. C. 16.

85 Vannovskaya O.V. op. cit. op. cit.

86 See: Sheretov V.V.. Criminological characterization of the personality of a bribe-taker [Electronic resource] - http://superinf.ru/view_helpstud.php?id=3005http://superinf.ru/view_helpstud. php?id=3005

norms is predominantly frivolous, which under certain conditions may lead to the commission of an act of bribery.

Personal psychological characteristics largely determine measures to combat corruption crime, the main ones being:

- formation of negative public opinion;
- Creating a negative attitude in those who give and those who take a bribe;
- psychological training for those who experience psychological pressure when extorting a bribe (representatives of small businesses, etc.);
- anti-corruption and legal education of the younger generation.

The implementation of these measures can have a significant impact on the formation of a sustainable rejection of corruption in society.

MIX
Papier aus verantwortungsvollen Quellen
Paper from responsible sources
FSC® C105338

Printed by Books on Demand GmbH, Norderstedt / Germany